The Associated Press Library of
disasters

Air, Sea, and Train Disasters

Grolier Educational

SHERMAN TURNPIKE, DANBURY, CONNECTICUT

Published 1998 by Grolier Educational, Danbury, CT 06816
This edition published exclusively for the school and library market

The publisher gratefully acknowledges permission from AP/Wide
World Photos to reproduce photographs.

A Creative Media Applications Production

Michael Burgan, Writer—Civil Unrest and Terrorism,
Tornadoes and Cyclones, Air, Sea, and Train Disasters,
and Nuclear and Industrial Disasters

Robin Doak, Writer—Earthquakes and Tsunamis,
Volcanoes, Wild Weather, and Fires and Explosions

Matt Levine, Editor

Alan Barnett, Inc., Design and Production

Lynne Karmen, Indexer

Set ISBN 0-7172-9169-3
Volume 6 ISBN 0-7172-9174-X

The Associated Press library of disasters.
        p.   cm.
        Includes indexes.
        Contents: v. 1. Earthquakes and tsunamis—v. 2. Civil unrest
and terrorism—v. 3. Volcanoes—v. 4. Tornadoes and cyclones—
v. 5. Wild weather—v. 6. Air, sea, and train disasters—
v. 7. Fires and explosions—v. 8. Nuclear and industrial disasters.
        ISBN 0-7172-9171-5 (v. 1 : hardbound).—ISBN 0-7172-9177-4
(v. 2 : hardbound).—ISBN 0-7172-9172-3 (v. 3 : hardbound).—
ISBN 0-7172-9175-8 (v. 4 : hardbound).—ISBN 0-7172-9170-7
(v. 5 : hardbound).—ISBN 0-7172-9174-X (v. 6 : hardbound).—
ISBN 0-7172-9173-1 (v. 7 : hardbound).—ISBN 0-7172-9176-6
(v. 8 : hardbound)
        1. Natural disasters—Juvenile literature. 2. Disasters—Juvenile
literature. [1. Natural disasters. 2. Disasters.] I. Associated
Press. II. Grolier Educational (Firm)
GB5019.A85 1997
363.34—dc21   97—26422
                                                    CIP
                                                    AC

Contents

Preface

Throughout the history of humankind there has always been the potential for disastrous events to take place over which people have little control. Cultures everywhere have continually sought to minimize the risk of disaster—and the destruction disaster can bring. Yet even in this age of science and technology, people still experience terrible disasters.

Today, newspaper journalism plays a large role in informing the world when disaster strikes. The Associated Press (AP), the world's largest news service, contributes daily to news worldwide, using satellite transmissions to send and receive reports from around the globe. The books in this set examine many different types of disasters in the 20th century, mainly as related through AP news articles and photos.

News articles often provide excellent coverage of disasters, but many disasters are never reported in the news. Those that occur during wartime are often kept secret by governments that do not wish their enemies to know of their troubles. Such disasters are not commonly known until years after they take place. Other disasters are poorly covered in the news if they happen in remote areas far from more populated regions. When reporters do not have access to these areas, it becomes impossible for them to write about such disasters.

This set uses a variety of articles to explore 20th-century disasters. Some of these were written with racial or cultural overtones that reflect feelings of people at the time of a disaster; these are not necessarily attitudes that prevail today. Likewise, some spellings and uses of language are different now than they were years ago. Original spellings and language are mostly kept as they were published within the articles.

One consequence of using news articles as an information source is that they are not always perfectly accurate. Occasionally, in a publisher's haste to get a news article into print, contradictory facts can be left within a single article. Furthermore, facts in one article can contradict facts in another. Finally, an article written shortly after a disaster may report what appear to be facts, but after investigations that can take weeks or even years, some of these "facts" may prove to be inaccurate. Supporting text before and after the articles in this set explains these inaccuracies, where possible.

Disasters are listed chronologically within each volume. Before each article headline is the date the article first appeared in a news source. Additionally, the set index included at the end of each volume can help readers locate particular disasters. For example, certain explosions directly related to nuclear or industrial accidents are located in Volume 8, *Nuclear and Industrial Disasters*, rather than in Volume 7, *Fires and Explosions*. Distinctions between different types of disasters are made in the introductions of the volumes, but the set index can help readers quickly find specific disasters within the set.

AIR, SEA, AND TRAIN DISASTERS

The Captain Doesn't Always Go Down with the Ship

The Portuguese were the first Europeans to sail far beyond their own continent to explore the world, and they were known as able seamen. One Portuguese captain, however, was more famous for his reckless ways and heavy drinking than his fine seamanship. This notorious sailor, whose name was unrecorded, captained the sailing ship *St. James* on its last voyage.

In the spring of 1586 the *St. James*, with more than 500 people on board, rounded the Cape of Good Hope off the southern tip of Africa. In a heavy wind and in the dead of the night the captain kept the ship running at full speed as it approached the island of Madagascar. Ignoring pleas to sail more carefully, the captain crashed his ship on some reefs near the island. The passengers panicked as the wooden ship began to break up on the rocks. The captain, knowing which of the ship's lifeboats were safest, escaped into one of those seaworthy craft and left the passengers to fend for themselves.

As the *St. James* went down, some passengers managed to repair one of the leaky lifeboats and head for safety. Desperately, hundreds tried to board the boat; the lucky ones already on board fought them off with knives and hatchets. Even then the lifeboat was overloaded, and as they sailed, the passengers threw off some of their shipmates. This lifeboat managed to reach the eastern coast of Africa, as did the captain's, and the survivors made their way back to Europe; but about 450 others perished in this *maritime*—or sea-related—disaster.

The Urge to Travel

The wreck of the *St. James* was not history's worst transportation accident, but it highlights some of the factors that lead to these disasters. Large numbers of people traveling on the most technologically advanced vehicles of the day put their trust in trained experts, but human error, natural elements, or both factors bring about a fatal end.

Although technology can improve safety for travelers, it can also increase the size of transportation disasters. More than double the number of people killed on the *St. James* died in some 20th-century maritime accidents, when bigger ships carried thousands of passengers. Steady increases in the size and speed of trains and planes have also created disasters with huge death tolls.

The need to travel, however, is strong, and people weigh the safety risks involved against the benefits: commercial activity, military conquest, interaction with other cultures, and the exploration of new lands. These goals stirred early humans to leave their homes and travel—first on foot, then relying on the power of animals. Today, technology has made it easier for people to cover great distances, and they often use the three modes of mass transportation examined in this book: ships, railways, and aircraft.

Taking to the Seas

Thousands of years ago people realized their lifestyles and freedom would be limited if they couldn't cross rivers or sail on lakes. The first shipbuilders lashed together pieces of wood to make rafts or hollowed out tree trunks to create canoes. Even the skins of dead animals were inflated and used as rowboats for short journeys.

The ancient Egyptians built the first large ships to transport goods across an empire that covered northern Africa and parts of the Middle East. These ships used both wind power (sails) and human power (oars). After the Egyptians every great culture around the world developed ships to haul people and cargo over the seas, but the conquering of water barriers was not complete; nature and human error could still deal disastrous blows. Huge storms capsized ships. Unseen rocks below the water's surface ripped holes in the bottoms of vessels, letting water rush in and sending the boats to the ocean floor. Fires broke out, torching wooden ships in minutes. In the 19th century, when ships switched from sails to steam power, steam engines exploded, and the introduction of steel still did not completely eliminate the hazard

of fire. Even skilled sailors could not avoid all these obstacles, and unskilled sailors heightened the risks of disasters at sea.

Over time sailors and scientists invented tools that improved maritime safety. Compasses kept ships on their desired courses, and maps showed where rocks threatened safe passage. The Chinese invented bulkheads, which were watertight sections of a ship that could be closed off, keeping water in one area before it filled the entire ship. Lifeboats—despite the example of the *St. James* above—allowed passengers and crew to escape a ship in distress.

In modern times radios let ships signal quickly for help during an emergency. Radar tracks ships at sea and guides them into port, but radar and on-board computers have not always prevented ships from ramming into each other or running aground. Safety equipment, like any machinery, can break down, and human negligence can add to the problem. Further, even the best weather forecasting doesn't keep some captains and shipping companies from sailing their ships through deadly storms.

Riding the Rails

In the 16th century German miners found an easy way to move large quantities of coal. First they built wooden rails leading out of the mines. Next they made wheels designed to roll on the rails and attached them to coal cars. Horses or humans then pulled the cars along the tracks. These were the first railways. Similar railways were later used to carry other goods, and in the 18th century King Louis XIV of France built a small railway at his palace for pleasure rides with his friends.

The railway's real impact, however, came in the 19th century, with the introduction of steam power. In 1804 Richard Trevithick, an English engineer, built the first steam engine to run on rails. About 20 years later the world's first public railway opened, designed to carry coal. Eventually the railroad's owners realized they could use their train to carry passengers too. On its first passenger run the train pulled about 80 tons of cargo and people at an average speed of 8 miles per hour. Transportation had entered a new era.

The United States was quick to catch up in railroad development, with its first passenger train running in 1830. The country also had its first recorded train accident six months later. The steam boiler on the *Best Friend of Charleston* exploded, killing the fireman. Steam engines could carry heavier loads at faster speeds than the old horse-drawn rail cars, but no one had ever died from an exploding horse!

Despite the risks of rail travel, trains spread across the U.S. and every country that industrialized during the 19th century. The railroads helped fuel the fortunes of American tycoons such as Jay Gould and Cornelius Vanderbilt, and they helped America settle its western lands. Better rails and steam engines led to faster trains, and traveling by train became common, but the improved technology led to even greater disasters.

During the rush to build more railways shoddy material or a lack of foresight often led to trouble. Trains plunged down embankments or into rivers when bridges could not hold the weight crossing them. Mismanagement of busy railway stations or tracks led to head-on collisions, nicknamed "cornfield meets." Embers from the coal stoves heating the cars could spark fires. Engineers found ways to improve rail safety, but not before hundreds of passengers had died.

The safety refinements included steel cars, which reduced the risk of fire, and the air brake, which allowed trains to stop quickly in an emergency. The telegraph helped improve communications along the railway, reducing fatal collisions, and electric and diesel engines replaced steam power, eliminating the risk of exploding boilers.

Today, in some poorer countries older equipment and rails still sometimes lead to train accidents that kill hundreds of people. Death tolls also tend to be high in places where trains—as opposed to cars or planes—are used as a major form of transportation, such as India. In most instances, however, rail travel is extremely safe, even as speeds of passenger trains approach 250 miles per hour.

Eye on the Sky

The myths of ancient civilizations are filled with stories of gods who could fly, whether on the backs of birds or magical flying animals, or on chairs with wings. Seeing birds in flight all around them, people long fantasized about taking to the skies themselves.

It took thousands of years before human knowledge and technology caught up with imagination, and humans finally rose off the earth. Balloons were the first vehicles that helped people fly. On September 19, 1783, two French brothers, the Montgolfiers, used hot-air balloons to launch animals into the sky. A month later an associate of theirs became the first passenger in a balloon.

Through the 19th century inventors developed balloons filled with gases that were lighter than air. When powered by engines, they could be steered during flight. These *dirigibles,* or airships, ushered in the first era of human flight, but they were not enough to satisfy the desire to fly. Engineers wanted to invent "heavier-than-air" craft—vehicles that could actually fly, rather than simply floating, as the balloons and airships did. They wanted to create air vessels with wings, just as medieval thinkers such as Roger Bacon and Leonardo da Vinci had envisioned. Gliders let pilots soar like birds, but they were limited in how far they could fly and how much weight they could carry. Combining the fixed wings of a glider with an engine, Orville and Wilbur Wright made the first successful airplane flight in 1903. Their invention would eventually let people travel farther and faster than ever before.

It took only five years after the Wright brothers' historic flight for the first airplane fatality to occur. While demonstrating the airplane to U.S. officials, Orville Wright and a passenger, Thomas E. Selfridge, crashed in Fort Myer, Virginia. Selfridge did not survive the crash.

The new airplane technology was obviously risky, and the chances for disaster grew after World War I as more people flew. The war had established the plane as an efficient weapon; now governments explored peaceful uses for planes. France and Great Britain introduced the first passenger services, but these ventures lost money. In the U.S. commercial aviation developed around the air transport of mail. Carrying passengers was an afterthought. In the 1920s pilots didn't need licenses or regulated training, and few people trusted this new technology for personal travel. In 1926 American planes carried just 5,800 passengers.

The successful transatlantic flight of Charles Lindbergh in 1927 fueled new interest in air travel. In the 1930s the first real commercial airlines began, as planes became bigger, safer, and more comfortable. Dirigibles, which had been used for commercial flights, faded from the scene. The development of jet engines in World War II led to even larger planes, and more people flew regularly.

Once again, however, advances in technology also led to greater disasters. In 1953 the world's first plane crash with more than 100 fatalities occurred outside Tokyo, Japan. Three years later the first major midair crash featured two U.S. planes colliding over the Grand Canyon. Unlike ships, planes had no lifeboats to improve the odds of surviving a midair calamity.

As with ships and trains, safety measures for planes improved. Most crashes happened during landings or takeoffs, so airports were modernized. Now computers help control the traffic near the ground and ease the landing process. Planes have special systems that prevent ice from forming on sensitive equipment during bad weather or at high altitudes. Inside, the cabins have oxygen masks and life preservers in case an accident does occur.

Statistically, planes are safer than automobiles.

For every 100 million passenger-miles flown per year (the number of passengers multiplied by the number of miles they fly), fewer than one passenger dies in an accident. About half of all aviation accidents, however, are caused by human error. This human factor—which suggests the accidents are preventable—and the often high death tolls make these disasters gripping events.

The Final Frontier

Once humans learned how to fly a few miles above Earth's surface, they raised their sights to outer space. Although the number of space disasters has been few, with a total of just fourteen fatalities, the explosion of the space shuttle *Challenger* drew enormous national and international attention and is included in this book with air disasters (see page 80).

The space age for humans dates back to 1961 and the flight of Russian cosmonaut Yuri Gagarin. The Soviet Union and the United States had been racing to put a human into space since 1957, with the launching of the first satellite, the Soviet craft *Sputnik*. Although the Soviets beat the Americans with *Sputnik* and Gagarin's flight, the ultimate first went to the United States. On July 20, 1969, American astronauts Neil Armstrong and Buzz Aldrin became the first humans to walk on the moon.

The conquest of space is one of the greatest technological achievements ever. That may be why failures in space seem so traumatic, even though they are so rare and not as deadly as a huge shipwreck or plane crash might be. Space accidents remind people that even the best minds and strongest efforts cannot eliminate the risks of modern transportation.

Notable Transportation Disasters before 1900

July 1502	Off Hispaniola	Spanish fleet destroyed by hurricane; 500 deaths
Spring 1586	Off the Cape of Good Hope	Wreck of the Portuguese sailing ship *St. James;* 450 deaths
July 1588	Off Ireland	Spanish warship *Gran Grifon* smashes into rocks; 1,000 deaths
1656	Caribbean Sea	Collision of two Spanish ships; 650 deaths
August 22, 1711	Off Labrador	Five English transport ships lost in bad weather; 2,000 deaths
1770	Off Chile	French ship *L'Orriflame* sinks in bad weather; 700 deaths
May 15, 1787	Caribbean Sea	British slave ship *Sisters* sinks in heavy winds; 500 deaths
December 24, 1811	Off Nova Scotia	British ships *St. George* and *Defence* lost in a gale; 2,000 deaths
July 15, 1864	Shohola, Pennsylvania	Head-on train collision; 148 deaths
April 26, 1865	Mississippi River	Paddle-wheel steamship *Sultana* explodes; 1,547 deaths
November 17, 1874	Off New Zealand	British frigate *Cospatrick,* carrying immigrants to New Zealand, catches fire; 468 deaths
January 11, 1879	Philippopolis, Turkey (now Plovdiv, Bulgaria)	Train bridge collapses; 200 deaths
June 24, 1881	Cuartla, Mexico	Train bridge collapses and train plunges into river; 216 deaths

Fire on the *General Slocum*

**East River, New York, New York
June 15, 1904
Death Toll: 1,021**

Paddle-wheel steamships were common in 19th-century America. Huge wooden paddles on either the rear or the sides of a ship were powered by steam engines, propelling these massive craft up and down the country's rivers.

Although often associated with the Mississippi River, paddle steamers also sailed in the East. The wooden paddle steamer *General Slocum* was a familiar site in New York. Launched in 1891, the *General Slocum* carried groups to picnics and other outdoor excursions outside New York City. On June 15, 1904, about 1,500 people, mostly German immigrants, boarded the *Slocum*. The ship never reached its destination on Long Island.

June 16, 1904

The Gen. Slocum Burned; 600 Dead

Had Picnic Party Aboard—Beached on Island in East River

Panic-Stricken Women and Children Burned to Death or Drowned

Fire Started in Lunch Room and Swept the Boat—
Upper Deck Burns and Falls, Crushing Many—
Men and Women Fight for Their Lives—Scores of
Blackened Bodies Recovered—Life Preservers Too Firmly
Fastened to Be Removed—Frantic Mothers Throw Children
Overboard or Jump With Them—500 Bodies Recovered

New York, June 15.—One of the most appalling disasters in the history of New York was that of to-day in the East River within a short distance of the New York shore and within sight of thousands of persons, when by the burning to the water's edge of the General Slocum, a three-decked excursion steamer, the largest in these waters, more than 600 persons, the majority of whom were women and children, were burned to death or drowned by jumping overboard, or by being thrown into the whirlpools by the lurching of the vessel.

Approximately 500 bodies have been recovered and are now being tagged at the morgues of Bellevue Hospital and Harlem. Divers were still busy at a late hour to-night taking bodies from the hold of the vessel, which they say is choked with bodies and those of hundreds who leaped or were thrown into the river have not been recovered.

Great preparations had been made for the seventeenth annual excursion of the Sunday school of St. Mark's German Lutheran Church, the congregation of which is drawn from the dense population of the Lower East and West sides, and the General Slocum had been chartered to carry the excursionists to Locust Grove, one of the many resorts on Long Island Sound.

Many Children on Board

It is variously estimated that there were between 1,500 and 2,500 persons on board the General Slocum when she left the pier at Third street, East River, though the Knickerbocker Steamboat Company, which owns the steamer, officially states that the number of passengers was 873, that being only one-third of the vessel's capacity. It is thought, however, that there were several hundreds of young children for whom fares are not usually charged on these excursions.

The excursion was in charge of Rev. George C.F. Haas, pastor of the church. The vessel was commanded by Captain William Van Schaick, one of the best known excursion boat captains in New York harbor, who has commanded the General Slocum almost since she was built in 1891.

The steamer proceeded up the East River, each of her decks being crowded with merrymakers, with bands playing and flags flying.

Fire Started in Lunch Room

She had reached a point at the Sunken Meadows, off One Hundred and Thirty-fifth street, which is at the extreme eastern end of Randall's Island, when fire started in a lunch room on the forward deck, caused by the overturning of a pot of grease. A high wind fanned the blaze into instant fury.

Efforts to subdue the fire were futile, and word was sent at once to the captain, who started to make a landing at One Hundred and Thirty-fourth street. At One Hundred and Thirty-fourth street there are several lumber yards and oil tanks and, as Captain Van Schaick started to turn his vessel towards the shore there, he was warned that it would set fire to the lumber and oil and so he changed his course for North Brother Island, one of the twin islands near the entrance to the Sound, some half mile away, where the boat was beached and after burning to the water's edge, sank at 12:25 o'clock, two hours and twenty-five minutes after the fire was discovered.

Couldn't Get at Life Preservers

In the meantime, the passengers had become panic-stricken and those who were not caught by the flames rushed to the stern of the vessel, where hundreds jumped overboard into the swiftly running water. It is alleged that the life preservers were too securely fastened to their holdings to be available and stories are told of frantic efforts by strong men to cut them loose; but even if they could have been torn down, they were too high up for the children to reach them. It is also alleged that no attempt was made to get out the fire apparatus at the first cry of "fire," though Captain Van Schaick says that he immediately rang the bells for getting out the apparatus. According to several statements, no attempt was made to lower boats or life rafts.

Race to North Brother Island

The race to North Brother Island was horribly dramatic. It was while the flames, which had now been fanned into a fury by the strong head wind, were consuming hundreds, both old and young. The scene was one of frightful panic, with men, women and children jumping overboard and being lashed by the whirlpools of the channel against the vessel's sides.

Men Fought with Women

Mothers and children became separated and frantically sought each other while in several cases fathers and mothers, gathering their children together, jumped with them into the water. Little children holding each other by the hand jumped together and were afterwards found clasped in each others arms. It is alleged that men fought with women to escape, resulting in the trampling under foot of scores of children.

Threw Children Overboard

The steamer's whistle was blowing for assistance, and tugs and other nearby craft answered the call. Before any of the boats could reach the burning steamer, however, the frantic women and children began to jump overboard. From the shore women could be seen hurling their children into the river, and with blazing dresses leaping after them.

The current was strong and there are many whirlpools in the channel. The boats that were following the Slocum picked up many from the water, but these were only a small number of those that were seen struggling in the swift current.

Deck Burned Away

On the Slocum the first sweep of the flames cut off escape from the hurricane deck, where a great many of the women and children were crowded together, and soon burned away the light woodwork which supported the deck. It is thought that most of those who were on this deck were burned.

As the fire increased, the struggle to gain a point of vantage at the stern became frightful, women and children crowded against the after rail until it gave way and hundreds were pushed off into the river. After this there was a steady stream of those who jumped or were thrown into the water. The tugs and small craft following kept close within the wake of the Slocum and rescued all of those who came within reach of their crews. Few of those who were saved had on life preservers. At no time during the progress of the fire was there any opportunity either to lower the life boats or get the life preservers out from underneath the seats.

Through all the wild panic the officers and men of the blazing boat stood at their posts.

Captain Saved

Captain William Van Schaick was among those saved. He jumped overboard with the rest when it was seen that the steamboat was doomed. According to one story, the captain was in the wheelhouse at the time the fire started and gave orders to the mate and crew to fight it. Those who had been in the kitchen when the fire started had to run for their lives, and when the mate and crew got to the kitchen the fire was beyond control. Captain Van Schaick was soon driven from the wheelhouse. Whatever attempt was made to enforce discipline was of no avail.

The burned wreck of the General Slocum *lies beached after the deadly fire that swept through the ship in June 1904.*

Hurricane Deck Falls

The Slocum got within fifty feet of the northwest point of North Brother Island and there stopped in shallow water. Just before she was beached the hurricane deck, the supports of which had burned away, fell with its load of women and children, overwhelming the crowd on the deck below. Very soon after parts of the second and third decks also caved in.

But before this happened the tug Water Tracy had come alongside the burning steamer and made fast to her. Many of the passengers were taken off by the crew of the Tracy, which remained alongside the steamer until the tug's pilothouse took fire.

The point where the Slocum was beached was just off the Scarlet Fever ward on North Brother Island. The patients, who had been out on the porches and lawns watching the approach of the burning steamer, were ordered indoors, and the physicians on the island hastened to the assistance of those who were being brought ashore through the shallow water. Many of those who leaped from the Slocum were carried away by the current even here and were drowned....

Boats to the Rescue

Among the boats that hurried to the aid of the stricken passengers were several tugs of the New York Central & Hudson River Railroad Company, the auxiliary catboat Easy Times, the health department tug Franklin Edson and the charities department Massasoit. These, with a swarm of rowboats manned by willing hands, approached as near the blazing vessel as was possible and rescued scores of people.

The Franklin Edson went so close to the burning steamer that her own paint was scorched. The crew of the tug, however, stuck bravely to their work and snatched many women and children from a terrible death. The fire had possession of the boat from stem to stern by the time she was off One Hundred and Thirty-eighth street. The fireboat Zophar Mills was summoned from her moorings at the foot of East Ninety-ninth street and was soon on the scene, its crew lending valuable aid in saving life.

Crowds at the Morgue

To-night a surging crowd is held back by police lines formed about the city morgue at the foot of East Twenty-sixth street. The crowd began to gather as soon as it became rumored about the city that the dead would be brought to Manhattan from North Brother Island and other places where at first they had been taken. When the Massasoit came to dock with eighty-five dead, the work of removing the bodies from the steamer proceeded slowly until no more room was found inside the morgue and the autopsy room was cleared and the blackened and distorted bodies were placed on the floor there.

When finally the morgue authorities allowed the crowd to enter the morgue, a scene ensued which was harrowing in the extreme. In some cases first identifications would be found to have been erroneous, men laying claim to bodies they afterwards discovered were not those of their relatives.…

■ ■ ■

Captain William Van Schaick had encountered trouble before on the *General Slocum*. In 1894 the ship had run aground, and seven years later a riot had broken out on board, injuring dozens. The 1904 fire led to many questions about Van Schaick and his crew's response to the disaster.

June 18, 1904

Probing the Slocum Disaster

Inspector Declines to Tell of Last Inspection

Says It Might Tend to Incriminate Him

Chief Engineer Tells His Story—Blazing Boat
Ran Four Miles Before It Was Beached

New York, June 17.—General Uhler of Washington, supervising inspector general of steamboats, Collector Stranahan, General Clarkson, the surveyor of the port, and local Supervising Inspectors Rodie and Dumont had a conference this afternoon and arranged for the inquiry into the Slocum disaster, which has been ordered by Secretary Cortelyou.

The session was secret, but it was learned that the character of the life preservers and fire equipment of the General Slocum received long consideration.

Collector Stranahan asked General Dumont to produce Inspector Lundberg, who had certified to the satisfactory equipment of the vessel. General

Dumont said that Lundberg was then appearing before Coroner Berry, but would be produced later as a witness.

When Inspector Lundberg appeared before Coroner Berry, he was accompanied by counsel. The coroner asked him several questions about his work, which he answered.

"When did you last inspect the Slocum?" asked Coroner Berry.

"I decline to answer that question by advice of counsel."

"On what grounds?" asked the coroner.

"On the grounds that it might tend to incriminate me," responded the inspector.

That ended the preliminary inquiry.

Blazing Boat Ran Four Miles

Statements were made to the coroner to-day by several of the employees, who will appear as witnesses at the inquest Monday, that the captain of the General Slocum sent his boat a distance of between three and four miles before beaching her. Several watches showed that more than half an hour had elapsed from the start of the fire until the boat was run ashore, all the watches which were taken from bodies of the drowned stopping between 10:10 and 10:20.

John J. Coakley, a deckhand, and the first man to reach the fire, said to-day that the General Slocum was near Blackwell's Island light when the fire started. This light is opposite East Eighty-sixth street, so that the fire must have started sooner than has heretofore been known, and nearly four miles from where the vessel was beached.

Coakley said that in his opinion the fire started in hay that was used in packing barrels of glassware

Standpipe Not Used

There is in the coroner's possession a standpipe taken, at his direction, by a diver from the submerged wreck. The valve of the pipe is closed tight, showing that no use was made of this pipe in fighting the flames on the General Slocum.

Two members of the crew of the Slocum to-day told their stories to the coroner. They denied that the firehose on board was rotten. They said it was twisted and that the pressure broke it.

One of the worst features of the disaster was the rottenness of many of the life preservers. There is abundant proof of their uselessness. Some which were taken from the bodies of the drowned were thrown over the sea wall at North Brother Island and sank out of sight at once. This matter is to be thoroughly investigated....

Chief Engineer's Story

B.F. Conlin, chief engineer of the General Slocum, is at his home in Catskill, N.Y., ill from the effects of his terrible experience in the disaster, but to-day he had so far recovered that he was able to talk about it. He did not know how the fire started, but said that while he was talking to his assistant, Everett Brandow, when opposite One Hundred and Thirty-eighth street, the first mate reported the fire. Mr. Conlin continued: "I at once ordered him to lay the hose while I went to the pumps, first notifying the captain, who was in the pilothouse, by calling to him through the speaking tube. I told Brandow to stand near the engine and not to leave it, and he obeyed me.

"In less than a minute water was being poured on the flames, but it did not seem to check them in the least. Two minutes or so later the fire alarm sounded and someone on deck cried 'fire.'

"Instantly there was a roar as the terrified passengers arose like one person and made a rush for the stern. Most of the crew were busy fighting the fire, and those who were on deck were unable to calm the fears of the women and children. The captain rang the bell for a full head of steam and the boat shot forward.

"At intervals the captain called through the speaking tube asking how the fire was progressing, and Brandow kept him informed. I stayed at the pumps, for I did not dare leave them, fearing that they might break down or stop. When the boat was beached and I left the engine room they were still working. If the hose was rotten and burst, as has been stated, I knew nothing of it, for the pumps worked regularly.

"Just before the Slocum was beached the engine room was in flames, and the large mirrors in it fell with a crash. I looked for Brandow and he was still standing near the throttle, with the flames all about him. The heat was intense. Brandow was badly burned about the head and neck, but he escaped. He and I were the last of the crew to leave the boat...."

■ ■ ■

Investigators finally determined that the fire had originated in a supply room filled with hay, oily rags, and other flammable material, though they weren't sure how the blaze had started. Captain Van Schaick was eventually arrested for manslaughter and for failing to properly train his crew in emergency procedures. He was convicted and sentenced to ten years in prison. In 1908 President Theodore Roosevelt pardoned the elderly captain.

President Roosevelt also ordered an investigation into the accident. A federal commission recommended that all new boats be built out of steel and have fireproof walls, but those suggestions came too late for the passengers of the *General Slocum.*

Today, a cemetery in Middle Village, New York, has a monument honoring the 1,021 victims of the *General Slocum* fire. Each year on June 15 a memorial service is held in their honor.

Sinking of the *Titanic*

Off the Coast of Newfoundland, Canada
April 14, 1912
Death Toll: 1,517

The great era of transatlantic travel began in the late 19th century. Steel replaced wood in the construction of ship hulls, and electricity lighted up the decks at night. Steamship lines competed with each other to build the largest and most luxurious ships afloat. By 1912 there was a new contender for the world's biggest and greatest ship: the *Titanic.*

Almost 900 feet long and weighing 45,000 tons, the *Titanic* was as grand as a royal palace and featured the latest maritime technology of the day. Its twelve watertight bulkheads, the ship's owners said, made the *Titanic* "unsinkable." The only thing the ship seemed to lack was enough lifeboats for its passengers and crew, but no regulations required ocean liners to provide lifeboats for everyone on board.

On April 10, 1912, some of the world's wealthiest people boarded this "unsinkable" ship for its first ocean voyage, which also turned out to be its last.

April 15, 1912

White Star Liner Titanic, Biggest Steamship Afloat, Strikes Iceberg on First Trip and is Sinking

Women Being Put Off In Life Boats—The Allan Liner Virginian Gets Wireless Call For Help and Proceeds To Aid Of Sinking Ship

Collision Off Cape Race—The Virginian 170 Miles Away and Will Not Reach the Titanic Till 10 A.M. Today— Titanic Sinking By the Head

Bulletin—Cape Race, N.F., Apr. 15.—At 10:25 o'clock last night the steamship Titanic called "S.O.S." and reported having struck an iceberg. The steamer said that immediate assistance was required.

Half an hour afterwards another message came reporting that they were sinking by the head and that women were being put off in the lifeboats.

Weather Clear

The weather was calm and clear, the Titanic's wireless operator reported, and gave the position of the vessel 41:46 north latitude and 50:14 west longitude.

The Marconi station at Cape Race notified the Allan liner Virginian, the captain of which immediately advised that he was proceeding for the scene of the disaster.

The Virginian at midnight was about 170 miles distant from the Titanic and expected to reach the vessel about 10 a.m. Monday.

The Olympic at an early hour Monday morning was in latitude 40:32 north and longitude 61:18 west. She was in direct communication with the Titanic and is now making all haste toward her.

Baltic Also to the Scene

The steamship Baltic also reported herself as about 200 miles east of the Titanic and was making all possible speed toward her.

The last signals from the Titanic were heard by the Virginian at 12:27 a.m. The wireless operator on the Virginian says these signals were blurred and ended abruptly.

Many Ships Near

New York, April 15.—One assuring feature of the accident to the Titanic is that a large number of ships appear to be within the big liner's call. Besides the Virginian of the Allan Line, which appears to be the first to have heard of the Titanic's distress, and the White Star liners Baltic and Olympic, both of which were reported on the way to the scene, there is also the Cincinnati of the Hamburg-American Line and the Cunarder Mauretania, the Hamburg-American liner Prinz Adelbert, and the Amerika of the same line, and the North German Lloyd liner Prinz Friedrich Wilhelm, bound from this port to Plymouth, all of which and many smaller liners are shown on today's steamship chart as in the vicinity of Cape Race.

■ ■ ■

Icebergs often break off from the polar cap in the Arctic Ocean and drift south into the northern Atlantic Ocean. As the *Titanic* sailed southeast of Newfoundland, it had received reports from other ships about icebergs, but the sightings were hundreds of miles away from the *Titanic*. As a result, the crew of the great liner was caught by surprise when the ship hit the fatal iceberg. The *Titanic* merely grazed the berg, but that was enough contact to open a series of small gashes in the ship's hull.

The passengers, too, were surprised as the ship stopped in the water, then began to sink. Despite the lack of lifeboats people remained calm, even as they faced their deaths.

Thirty Men Saved On Floating Raft

Thrown Into Icy Water, They Were Kept Up By Bits of Wreckage

Army Officer's Graphic Story of His Escape

Helped to Drag Others On to Raft—Praises Bravery of Astor

New York, April 18.—Colonel Archibald Gracie, U.S.A., the last man saved, went down with the vessel, but was picked up. He was met tonight by his daughter, who had arrived from Washington, and his son in law, Paul H. Fabricius. Colonel Gracie told a remarkable story of personal hardship and denied emphatically the reports that there was any panic on board. He praised in the highest terms the behavior of both the passengers and crew and spoke especially of the heroism of the woman passengers.

Mrs. Straus Wouldn't Leave Husband

"Mrs. Isidor Straus," he said, "went to her death because she would not desert her husband. Although he pleaded with her to take her place in the boat, she steadfastly refused and when the ship settled at the head the two were engulfed by the wave that swept her."

Colonel Gracie described how he was driven to the topmost deck when the ship settled and how he was the sole survivor after the wave that swept her just before her final plunge had passed.

Jumped With Wave

"I jumped with the wave," said he, "just as I often have jumped with the breakers at the seashore. By great good fortune I managed to grasp the brass railing on the deck above, and I hung on by might and main. When the ship plunged down I was forced to let go and I was swirled around and around for what seemed to be an interminable time. Eventually I came to the surface, to find the sea a mass of tangled wreckage.

Seized Wooden Grating

"Luckily I was unhurt and casting about managed to seize a wooden grating for floating. When I had recovered my breath I discovered a larger canvas and cork life raft which had floated up. A man, whose name I did not learn, was struggling toward it from some wreckage to which he had clung. I cast off and helped him to get onto the raft and we then began the work of rescuing those who had jumped into the sea and were floundering in the water.

Thirty Survivors On Raft

"When dawn broke there were thirty of us on the raft standing knee deep in the icy water and afraid to move lest the cranky craft be overturned. Several unfortunates, benumbed and half dead, besought us to save them and one or two made an effort to reach us but we had to warn them away. Had we made any effort to save them we all might have perished. The hours that elapsed before we were picked up by the Carpathia were the longest and most terrible that I ever spent. Practically without any sensation of feeling because of the icy water, we were almost drooping from fatigue. We were afraid to turn around to look to see whether we were seen by passing craft and when someone who was facing astern passed the word that something that looked like a steamer was coming up one of the men became hysterical under the strain. The rest of us, too, were nearing the breaking point."

Revolver Fired Only Once

Colonel Gracie denied with emphasis that any men were fired upon and said that only once was a revolver discharged.

"This was to intimidate some steerage passengers," he said, "who had tumbled into a boat before it was prepared for launching. This shot was fired in the air, and when the foreigners were told that the next would be directed at them they promptly returned to the deck. There was no confusion and no panic."

Contrary to the general expectation, there was no jarring impact when the vessel struck, according to the army officer. He was in his berth when the vessel dashed into the submerged part of the berg and was aroused by the jar. He looked at his watch, he said, and found it was just midnight. The ship sank with him at 2:22 a.m. for his watch stopped at that hour.…

Woman Refused to Be Rescued

One of the last women seen by Colonel Gracie, he said, was Miss Evans of New York, who virtually refused to be rescued because, according to the army officer, "she had been told by a fortune teller in London that she would meet her death on the water."

The hull of the Titanic *lies on the bottom of the Atlantic Ocean, illuminated by a light from the research submarine* Alvin. *In 1986 scientist Robert Ballard used the sub to discover the* Titanic's *wreckage.*

Warnings Ignored

Colonel Gracie said that despite the warnings of icebergs, no diminution in speed was ordered by the commander of the Titanic. There were other warnings too, he said.

"In the twenty-four hours' run ending the fourteenth," he said, "the ship's run was 546 miles, and we were told that the next twenty-four hours would see even a better record posted. No diminution of speed was indicated in the run and the engines kept up their steady running. When Sunday evening came we all noticed the increased cold, which gave plain warning that the ship was in close proximity to icebergs or ice fields. The offi-

cers, I am credibly informed, had been advised by wireless from other ships of the presence of icebergs and dangerous floes in that vicinity. The sea was as smooth as glass, and the weather clear, so that it seems that there was no occasion for fear."

No Panic When She Struck

When the vessel struck, he continued, "the passengers were so little alarmed that they joked over the matter. The few that appeared on deck early had taken their time to dress properly and there was not the slightest indication of panic. Some of the fragments of ice had fallen on the decks and these were picked up and passed around by some of the facetious ones, who offered them as mementoes of the occasion. On the port side a glance over the side failed to show any evidence of damage and the vessel seemed to be on an even keel. James Clinch Smith and I, however, soon found the vessel was listing heavily."

■ ■ ■

Investigations after the sinking of the *Titanic* put the blame on Captain E.J. Smith and his officers for ignoring the earlier reports of icebergs. The disaster led to new safety regulations for ocean liners. Ships had to carry enough lifeboats for all the people on board, and passengers had to go through an emergency drill. Also, ships were required to staff their radio rooms 24 hours a day; some of the ships near the *Titanic* did not receive its distress signals because they had turned off their radios for the night.

The *Titanic's* sinking also led to the founding of the International Ice Patrol to monitor the movement of icebergs. Today, ships, planes, and satellites help track icebergs that drift into shipping lanes.

Almost 75 years after the disaster a team of American and French researchers found the remains of the *Titanic* almost 13,000 feet below the ocean's surface. In 1996 an attempt to raise part of the ship failed, but explorers have brought back artifacts from the *Titanic*. Some people, including Robert Ballard, the original discoverer of the remains, argue that the ship should be left alone, in tribute to the more than 1,500 victims.

Empress of Ireland-Storstad Collision

St. Lawrence River, Quebec, Canada
May 29, 1914
Death Toll: 1,014

In 1906 the Canadian Pacific Railway launched the *Empress of Ireland* and its sister ship, the *Empress of Britain*. The two liners sailed between England and Canada, carrying more than 1,000 passengers apiece.

On May 28, 1914, the *Empress of Ireland* left Quebec bound for Liverpool, England. The ship never reached the Atlantic Ocean, as it became the victim of the worst maritime disaster in Canadian history.

May 30, 1914

934 Lives Lost When Steamship Empress of Ireland, Stationary In Fog In St. Lawrence River, Is Rammed By Collier; Sinks In 14 Minutes

Steamer, In Sight of Shore, Is Struck By Collier Storstad and Her Side Is Ripped Open Clear to Stern—Passengers Asleep and Hundreds Were Unable to Reach Deck Before Vessel Went Down—Of the 433 Known to Have Been Saved 237 Were Members of Crew—Twenty-two of the Rescued Died From Injury Or Exposure—Survivors Overcome In Chilled Water Lose Hold of Wreckage and Are Drowned—Wireless Call Brings Quick Response, But Vessel Went Down At Once and Rescue Ships Saved Those Clinging to Lifeboats and Rafts

Only a Dozen Women Among the Saved

No Time to Cry "Women First"—Passengers Who Heard Frenzied Cry of Officers Rushed Up From Cabins In Scanty Attire—Explosion Quickly Followed the Collision and Catapulted People From Her Decks Into the Sea—Captain Kendall Stood On Bridge Until Ship Went Down, and Is Picked Up

Rimouski, P.Q., May 29.—Sinking in ninety feet of water within fifteen minutes after being rammed amidships in the upper reaches of the St. Lawrence River, early today, the Canadian Pacific liner Empress of Ireland carried down with her more than 900 of her passengers and crew. Of the 1,367 persons on board the liner, only 433 are known to have been saved, making the probable death list 934....

The rescued on board numbered 29 first class, 29 second class and 101 third class passengers and 237 of the crew. Thirty-seven survivors were left at Rimouski, which would make a total of 433 saved.

Crashed Bow On In Fog

Looming up through the river mists, as the Empress of Ireland was lying to, waiting for the fog to lift, or day to break, the Danish collier Storstad crashed bow on into the side of the big Canadian liner, striking her about midway of her length and ripping her side open clear to the stern.

The crash occurred not far from the shore off Father Point, 150 miles from Quebec, which the Empress of Ireland left yesterday afternoon, bound for Liverpool, and ten miles from this point on the St. Lawrence. In reality, therefore, although the liner was heading for the sea and the collier coming in from it, the disaster was not one of the ocean, but of the river. Unlike the Titanic's victims, the Empress of Ireland's lost their lives within sight of shore—in land-locked waters.

Wireless Call For Help

As soon as the ship's crew recovered from the shock of the collision and it was seen that the liner had received a vital blow, a wireless "SOS" call was sounded.

The hurried appeal was picked up by the government mail tender Lady Evelyn, here, and the government pilot boat Eureka, at Father Point, and both at once set out to the rescue.

So deep was the hurt of the Empress, however, and so fast the inrush of waters, that long before either of the rescue boats could reach the scene, the liner had gone down. Only floating wreckage and a few lifeboats and rafts from the steamer, buoying up less than a third of those who had set sail on her, were to be found.

Many Crushed to Death

The rest had sunk with the liner, had been crushed to death in the Storstad's impact with her, or had been forced from exhaustion and exposure in the ice-chilled northern waters to loose their hold on bits of wreckage and had drowned.

Only a few persons were picked up by the Storstad, which was badly crippled herself by the collision, and these were brought here by the collier, together with those saved by the Eureka and the Lady Evelyn.

Twenty-two of Rescued Died

Twenty-two of the rescued died from injury or exposure. The others, most of whom had jumped into the boats or plunged into the water from the sinking liner, scantily clad, were freely given such clothing as the town could supply, and later those who were well able to travel were put on board a train and started for Quebec, where they arrived tonight.

Went Down in Fourteen Minutes

Accounts agree that in the brief space of time— not more than fourteen minutes—between the shock of the collision and the sinking of the liner, there was little chance for systematic marshaling of the passengers. Indeed, everything indicates that hundreds of those on the steamer probably never reached the decks. Very few women were among the saved, not more than a dozen, the lists make it appear.

"It all happened so quickly that we did not really know what was going on, and nobody had time to cry 'women first,'" one of the passengers told Captain Bellinger of the rescue boat Eureka.

"The stewards did not have time to rouse the people from their berths," the survivor added. "Those who heard the frenzied calls of the officers for the passengers to hurry on deck lost no time in obeying them, rushing up from their cabins in scanty attire. They piled into the boats, which were rapidly lowered and were rowed away. Many who waited to dress were drowned."

Explosion Adds To Horror

The horror of the interval during which the Empress of Ireland was rapidly filling and the frightened throngs on board her were hurrying every effort to escape before she sank was added to by an explosion which quickly followed the collision. According to one of the rescued, the explosion, probably caused by the water reaching the boilers, bulged the liner's sides and catapulted people from her decks out into the sea. The ship made a heavy list as the water pouring in weighed her on the side where she was struck, and made the work of launching boats increasingly difficult from moment to moment, and when she finally took her plunge to the bottom, scores were still left on her decks, being carried down in the vortex, only a few being able to clear her sides and find support on pieces of wreckage.

Captain Kendall a Hero

From all accounts, Captain H.G. Kendall of the Empress of Ireland bore himself like a true sailor so long as his ship stood under him. He retained such command of the situation, it appears, that while the Storstad's stem still hung in the gash it had made in the Empress's side, Captain Kendall begged the master of the collier to keep his propellers going so that the hole might remain plugged. The Storstad, however, dropped back and the Empress filled and foundered.

Stood on Bridge as Ship Sank

Captain Kendall stood on his bridge as the ship went down. One of the boats from the liner picked him up and he directed its work of saving others until the craft was loaded to the gunwale. The captain was injured in the crash and suffered from exposure, but his hurts are not dangerous and his speedy recovery is expected.

Picking Up Survivors

When day broke this morning the rescue boats had not yet returned from the scene of the wreck. People standing on shore at Father Point scanned the horizon with telescopes, saw the rescue steamers picking up boats off in the river, and prepared to give help to the survivors. They were sorely in need of help, as most of them had on little clothing and the temperature was almost down to the freezing point. When they had been given attention and started on their way to Quebec, the work of recovering bodies was undertaken.

250 Bodies Recovered

The rescue steamers themselves had brought in nearly fifty of these and tonight after they had continued their search the entire day, a total of about 250 bodies had been recovered. One woman and four men, still living, but unconscious, were picked up during the day by the steamers. Few of the bodies had been identified tonight.

■ ■ ■

Unlike the *Titanic* (see page 11), the *Empress* had more than enough lifeboats on board for its passengers and crew, but after the collision the ship listed badly to one side, and only a few of its boats could be launched.

The day after the collision Captain Henry George Kendall offered his view on what had happened in the St. Lawrence River fog.

May 31, 1914

Empress' Captain Tells Story of Fatal Collision

Captain Kendall Says Fog Drifted Between His Ship and Collier Storstad, When Two Miles Apart—Stopped His Ship Dead and Whistled to Storstad That He Had Done So— Storstad Acknowledged Signal—Saw Port and Starboard Lights a Ship's Length Away—Captain Yelled Five Times Not to Back Off, But Keep Bow In Ripped Side of Steamer— Storstad Pulled Out and Empress Filled Rapidly

Blame Placed on Storstad

No Panic, Crew and Passengers Behaved Splendidly— Chief Engineer Dictates Testimony From Bed— Tells of Orders Which Came From Bridge— Final Count Shows 403 Rescued and 964 Lost

Rimouski, Que., May 30.—While final tabulations of the casualties in the sinking of the ill-fated steamer Empress of Ireland were being made today, showing that 403 of her passengers and crew had been rescued and 964 had perished, Captain Henry George Kendall of the liner was telling his story of the disaster, at an inquiry conducted by Coroner Pinault here.

Captain Kendall declared that he had taken all possible precaution against a collision. His ship had been stopped; he gave the requisite signals when the Danish collier Storstad, which dealt the blow which sent the Empress to the bottom, was still two miles away; but the collier had kept on through the fog which settled down soon after the two vessels sighted each other and had rammed the Empress of Ireland while the latter was virtually motionless. Then, despite his plea to the master of the collier that he run his engines full speed ahead to keep the hole in the liner's side plugged with the Storstad's bow, said Captain Kendall, the Danish vessel backed away, the water rushed in, and the Empress sank.

Stuck to Bridge

Captain Kendall, who stuck to the bridge of his ship to the last and after being picked up by a lifeboat aided in saving a boat load of drowning persons from the wreck, took up his story of the disaster from the point at which the Empress of Ireland, bound from Quebec for Liverpool, had dropped her pilot Thursday night at Father Point, near which the disaster of yesterday morning occurred.

At Full Speed

"We then proceeded full speed," continued Captain Kendall. "After passing Rock Point Gas Buoy I sighted the steamer Storstad, it then being clear.

Fog Came Up

"The Storstad was then about one point, twelve degrees on my starboard bow. At that time, I saw a slight fog bank coming gradually from the land and knew it was going to pass between the Storstad and myself. The Storstad was about two miles away at that time. Then the fog came and the Storstad's lights disappeared. I rang full speed astern on my engines and stopped my ship.

Signaled His Position

"At the same time I blew three short blasts on the steamer's whistle meaning 'I am going full speed astern.' The Storstad answered with the whistle, giving me one prolonged blast.

"I then looked over the side of my ship into the water and I saw my ship was stopped. I stopped my engines and blew two long blasts meaning 'My ship was under way but stopped and has no way upon her.' He answered me again with one prolonged blast. The sound was then about four points upon my starboard bow.

Saw Red and Green Lights

"It was still foggy. I looked out to where the sound came from. About two minutes afterward, I saw his red and green lights. He would then be about one ship's length away from me. I shouted to him through the megaphone to go full speed astern, as I saw the danger of collision was inevitable; at the same time I put my engines full speed ahead with my helm hard aport, with the object of avoiding, if possible, the shock. Almost at the same time he came right in and cut me down in a line between the funnels.

Storstad Backed Away

"I shouted to the Storstad to keep full speed ahead to fill the hole he had made. He then backed away. The ship began to fill and listed over rapidly. When he struck me, I had stopped my engines. I then rang full speed ahead again, when I saw the danger was so great, with the object of running her on shore to save passengers and ship. Almost immediately the engines stopped the ship filling and going over all the time, starboard.

Wireless Calls For Aid

"I had, in the meantime, given orders to get the lifeboats launched. I rushed along the starboard side of the boat deck and threw all the gripes out of numbers 1, 3, 5 and 7 boats; then I went back to the bridge again where I saw the chief officer rushing along to the bridge. I told him to tell the wireless operator at once to send out distress signals. He told me that this had been done. I said 'Get the boats out as quick as possible.' That was the last I saw of the chief officer. Then, in about three to five minutes after that, the ship turned over and foundered.

"I was shot into the sea myself from the bridge and taken down with the suction. The next thing I remember was seizing a piece of grating. How long I was on it, I do not know, but I heard some men shout from a lifeboat, 'There is the captain; let us save him.'

Aided Rescue Work

"They got to me and pulled me in the boat. The boat already had about thirty people in it. I did my best with the people in the boat to assist in saving others. We pulled around and picked up twenty or twenty-five more in the boat, and also put about ten around the side in the water with ropes around their wrists, hanging on. Seeing that we could not possibly save any more, we pulled to the Storstad which was then about a mile and a half away. I then got all these people put on board the Storstad and then left her with six of the crew, and went back and tried to save more. When we got there everybody had gone. We searched around and could not see anybody alive, so then we returned to the Storstad."

Storstad To Blame

"What was the cause of the collision?" asked the coroner.

"The Storstad running into the Empress, which was stopped," answered Kendall.

Captain Kendall, in answer to a question by a juror, said that when he shouted to the Storstad's captain to stand fast, he received no answer. It was impossible for him to have heard, he added.

"I shouted five times; I also shouted, 'Keep ahead,'" said Captain Kendall, "and if he did not hear that he should have done it, as a seaman should have known that."

"There was wind?"

"It was quite still.…"

Marine Engineer Testifies

James Rankin, a passenger from Vancouver, B.C., and a marine engineer, said:—

"I was aroused by the noise and ran out. There was a big pitch to the deck. I heard the whistle blow when I reached the deck. There was a heavy fog and you could hardly see fifty yards. Five minutes after the collision, the fog lifted. The boats on the lower side were in the water and four or five of them got away and saved many people.

Should Have Kept Bow in Hole

"I think that if the collier had kept her bow in the hole she had made in the Ireland's side, she would have been able to make the shore and probably have saved every one.

"The behavior of the officers on the Empress was beyond all praise. They did everything they could. The engineers remained below until they could get no more steam and the lights went out."

Chief Engineer's Story

Chief Engineer Sampson, who remained in the engine room until the fires were drowned and the lights extinguished, was too ill to appear, and his testimony was taken at his bedside.

"I was in the engine room until the lights went out and there was no more steam," he said. "I had great difficulty in reaching the decks, owing to the great list of the ship. No sooner had I got on deck when the boats of the portside, which had broken loose, swept down on top of us and carried us under water. When I came to the surface I found myself under a lifeboat and entangled in wreckage. I was finally pulled into one of the boats and could see the collier about a mile and a half away. Immediately before the collision, we went full speed astern and then stopped. Then I got the order full speed ahead, but had only started the engines when the crash came. We then kept her full speed ahead to try to reach the shore, as long as we had steam. Owing to the steam failing us, and then the lights also, we could keep the engines going for only a few minutes.

No Explosion

"There was no explosion of any kind. I saw no reason why the collier did not keep much closer than she did, as, if she had, there would have been many lives saved. I am also of the opinion that had she stuck to us we should have reached the shore.…"

■ ■ ■

The captain of the *Storstad,* Thomas Anderson, was held fully responsible for the disaster, and the Canadian Pacific Railway filed a $2 million legal claim against the ship's owners. Today, the *Empress of Ireland* remains at the bottom of the St. Lawrence River. Divers have failed in their attempts to salvage jewelry locked in the ship's safe.

Capsizing of the *Eastland*

Chicago River, Chicago, Illinois
July 24, 1915
Death Toll: 852

Like the people on the *General Slocum* (see page 7), the passengers on the steamer *Eastland* were prepared for a day of picnicking and festivity—but the *Eastland* never even left the docks.

July 25, 1915

1,000 Excursionists Drown as Steamer Capsizes;

842 Bodies Are In Temporary Morgue At Armory; Investigation Is Begun To Fix Blame For Tragedy

Eastland, Said to Have Been Topheavy, Turns Over In Chicago River With More Than 2,400 Employees of Western Electric Company, Relatives and Friends On Board

Scores Go Down, Almost Within Grasp Of River Bank

Thrilling Rescues Made by Divers, Policemen, Firemen and Volunteers—Countless Deeds of Heroism—Victims Taken To Armory Where Sad Identification Scenes Are Enacted

Chicago, July 24.—A thousand persons lost their lives in the Chicago River today by the capsizing of the excursion steamer Eastland while warping from its wharf with more than 2,400 employees of the Western Electric Company and their relatives and friends on board, bound for a pleasure trip across Lake Michigan.

After working ceaselessly all day and far into the night, the bodies of 842 victims of the catastrophe, most of them women and children, were collected from temporary morgues and taken to the Second Regiment Armory. When these bodies had been tagged, Coroner Hoffman, taking into consideration estimates of bodies thought to be in the hold of the steamer, lying on its side in the river, and in the stream itself, said he had hopes that the total dead would not exceed 1,000.

Said To Have Been Topheavy

The Eastland, said by marine architects to have been topheavy and ballasted in an uncertain manner, turned over inside of five minutes after it began to list, pouring its gala passengers into the river, or imprisoning them in its submerged hull.

Hundreds Drown Miserably

Every effort was made by thousands of persons on the river wharf to rescue the drowning men, women and children, but many drowned almost within grasp of the river bank. Mothers went to death while their children were snatched to safety. Other children died in the arms of their parents who were finally saved. Hundreds of girls, freed for a day from their tasks of making telephones and other electrical apparatus in the factory of the Western Electric Company, dressed in their smartest white frocks, drowned miserably.

Sorrow Over West Side

A pall of sorrow hung tonight over the entire west side of Chicago, where the majority of the victims lived. And many of the ill-fated residents of this district tonight lay in the morgue, or beneath the steel hull of the Eastland, over which searchlights shot their blinding glare while hundreds of men searched for more bodies.

Investigation Begun

Efforts to discover the cause of the accident were begun long before the work of rescue was over. Federal and county grand juries were ordered, a coroner's jury was empanelled and all the officers and crew of the Eastland were arrested.

Secretary Steele Arrested

W.C. Steele, secretary and treasurer of the St. Joseph Chicago Steamship Company, which owned the Eastland, built on Lake Erie in 1903 and remodeled later because it was topheavy, it is said, was arrested tonight and locked up at a police station. The steamer was leased by the Indiana Transportation Company, whose officers said they were not responsible for the licensing of the ship and did not control the crew.

7,000 Off for Excursion

Under misty skies 7,000 men, women and children wended their way to the Clark street dock early to fill five large lake steamers with holiday mirth and a trip to Michigan City. The steamer Eastland, brought to Chicago from Lake Erie after an unsatisfactory career, was the first to be loaded.

Rain began to fall as the wharf superintendents lifted the gangplanks from the Eastland, declaring that the government limit of 2,500 passengers had been reached. Those aboard waved goodbye to friends on shore waiting to board the steamer Theodore Roosevelt and other vessels.

Steamer Wavers Sidewise

Then the passengers swarmed to the left side of the ship as the other steamers drew up the river towards the wharf. A tug was hitched to the Eastland, ropes were ordered cast off, and the steamer's engines began to hum. The Eastland had not budged, however. Instead, the heavily laden ship wavered sidewise, leaning first towards the river bank. The lurch was so startling that many passengers joined the large concourse already on the river side of the decks.

The ship never heeled back. It turned slowly, but steadily, towards its left side. Children clutched the skirts of mothers and sisters to keep from falling. The whole cargo was impelled towards the falling side of the ship. Water began to enter lower portholes and the hawsers tore out the spiles to which the vessel was tied.

Screams as Eastland Goes Over

Screams from passengers attracted the attention of fellow excursionists on the wharf awaiting the next steamer. Wharfmen and picnickers soon lined the edge of the embankment, reaching out helplessly towards the steamer.

For nearly five minutes the ship turned before it finally dived under the swift current, which, owing to the drainage canal system, flows from the lake. During the turning of the ship with its cargo of humanity, lifeboats, chairs and other loose appurtenances on the decks skipped down the sloping floors, crushing the passengers towards the rising waters.

Hundreds Drown Miserably

Then came a plunge with a sigh of air escaping from the hold, mingled with crying of children and shrieks of women, and the ship was on the bottom of the river, casting hundreds of living creatures to the water.

Many sank, entangled with clothing and bun-

dles, and did not rise, but hundreds came to the surface and seized floating chairs and other objects. Those on shore threw out ropes and dragged in those who could hold the life lines. Employees of commission firms along the river threw crates, chicken coops and other buoyant things into the current, but most of these were swept away by the stream which runs five miles an hour.

Boats put out, tugs rushed to the scene with shrieking whistles, and many men snatched off coats and shoes and sprang into the river to aid the drowning. With thousands of spectators ready to aid and the wharf within grasp, hundreds went to death, despite every effort at rescue.

Many Incidents of Heroism

Instances of heroism were almost countless. One man clung to a spike in the side of the wharf while two women and three children stepped upon his body as on a ladder to safety. He fell exhausted into the river as the last one of the five reached the pier.

Boats, as soon as full, took rescued passengers to the wharf or to the steamer Theodore Roosevelt, which was tied up opposite the Eastland.

In an hour the water was cleared of excursionists. Those who had not been taken to land had sunk or were swirling down the river towards the drainage canal locks at Lockport, Ill., many miles away. The locks were raised to stop the current and arrangements were made to take bodies from the river along its course through the southwest part of Chicago.

Cut Into Hold With Gas Flames

Soon after the water was cleared, city firemen, ship engineers and helpers were on the exposed side of the Eastland's hull, cutting through its steel plates with gas flames. Divers were hurried into underwater suits. A tug was moored as a bridge between the pier and the capsized ship.

As the divers gained entrance to the hull, the scene of distress moved for the time being from the river to the extemporized morgues. Warehouses of wholesale companies along the river were thrown open and bodies were placed in rows on the floors. Scores of persons rescued from the water were injured and these were taken to the Iroquois Hospital, built in memory of the 600 women, children and a few men who were burned and crushed to death in the Iroquois Theater on New Year's eve several years ago.

Efforts to resuscitate those taken from the river were generally unsuccessful. Only two or three were thus saved. It was also said that many of the injured would die....

Divers Recover Corpses

While those on land were disposing of the dead, injured and rescued, the divers in the heart of the sunken vessel sent up an almost constant stream of corpses from the submerged decks. First it was a gaily dressed girl in her teens who had been caught between a pile of chairs and a cabin wall. Next it was a slight boy, gathered from the lifeless arms of a father who had clung to his offspring even in death. Then followed an old woman, who had gone aboard the ship to watch the youthful pleasure of her grandchildren, or a little girl with bare legs and bootees with gay ribbons sodden against the lace of her holiday gown....

Work of tagging the bodies of the dead and placing them in accessible places for identification proceeded all day and night. Reports from various temporary morgues became so confusing that it was decided to take all bodies to the Second Regiment Armory so that those who were looking for lost friends and relatives could view all the victims in one place....

■ ■ ■

Although the preceding news report describes workers using torches to cut through the *Eastland*'s hull, it leaves out a bizarre fact: Harry Pederson, the ship's captain, refused to let the men cut the hole, even as trapped survivors pounded on the inside. The workers ignored Pederson and went ahead with their efforts, rescuing 40 people.

After the disaster Illinois officials arrested the officers of the Indiana Transportation Company, the firm that had leased the *Eastland*. The charges of negligence went even higher, and President Woodrow Wilson sent representatives to the scene.

Many Bodies May Be Held Under Eastland's Hull

Steamer to be Righted and Pumped Out—Will Take Ten to Thirty Days—Plans for Three Probes Completed

Detectives Seize Excursion Tickets

Said to Show More Than 2,500 on Board—Chicago Officials Allege Federal Negligence—Dead May Reach 1,200

Chicago, Ill., July 26.—Plans for investigations by federal, state and city official bodies, to determine who was to blame for the capsizing of the steamer Eastland in the Chicago River Saturday with a loss of hundreds of lives, were completed tonight. A coroner's jury will start an inquest tomorrow while federal departments, headed by Secretary of Commence Redfield and Officers from the city police department and the office of State's Attorney Maclay Hoyne, will gather evidence, holding formal inquiry in abeyance until the inquest has progressed as far as possible.

Efforts were continued today to remove victims of the disaster from the wrecked ship and to determine whether the total death list would remain around 1,000, as many believed, or creep up to 1,200 or more, as others predicted. Registration of employees by the Western Electric Company showed nearly 400 missing, but many of the names of these were included in the list of 826 bodies already identified. It was said also that probably many did not report at the plant, although safe.

Tickets Seized

The probability of swelling the list above a thousand was suggested by the announcement of detectives from the state's attorney's office that they had seized the tickets taken from passengers boarding the Eastland for the excursion to Michigan City, Ind. They asserted that these tickets numbered 2,550 and did not account for children, musicians and the seventy-two members of the crew. They estimated that the total number of persons aboard the steamer might have been 2,800 or more, instead of the 2,480 previously announced by officers of the Indiana Transportation Company. The lessees of the ship asserted that 2,480 passenger tickets had been collected. State's Attorney Hoyne, in pursuing his investigation, tonight seized correspondence which had passed between officers of the Western Electric Employees' organization, which gave the picnic, and the Indiana Transportation Company, operating the Eastland and four other steamers set aside to carry more than 7,000 persons across the lake.

The state's attorney and this correspondence showed that the steamer company had advised that the more tickets sold, the greater would be the rebate paid to the employees' organization. Tickets were to be sold to employees of the Western Electric company for 75 cents at the factory, or $1 at the wharf. According to the state's attorney the letters showed there would be a rebate of one-third on all tickets over 4,000 and something less on those above 2,500.

Almost Forced to Buy Tickets

Complaint had already been made by several employees of the Western Electric Company that they had been almost compelled to buy tickets for the excursion by fear that officers of the employees' organization who sold them would discriminate against those who failed to go on the excursion. The picnic to Michigan City has been an annual affair, and these men said that employees who had refused to buy tickets in previous years had received less remunerative work or been discharged, probably without the sanction of executives of the company.

To the confusion of determining the total number of lives lost there was added much wrangling among officials of different jurisdiction over tentative plans to right the Eastland, which still lies on its port side where it sank.

Despite an all-day search of the hulk by divers and a constant dragging of the river bed between the wreck and a net stretched across the river a block down the current, only a dozen bodies were found. Estimates of the number still held under

water varied from 150 to 500. The steamer, with a width of thirty-eight feet, protruded twelve or thirteen feet above the river. This, divers said, indicated that the lower edge of the wreck did not sink more than a foot into the muddy bottom.

Rescue boats swarm around the Eastland *as passengers wait to leave the capsized ship.*

Not to Use Dynamite

Estimates by marine engineers showed that it would take from ten to thirty days to put the Eastland on its keel. It was said that until the ship was removed it could not be determined how many, if any, bodies had been caught under the hull and superstructure. Plans to use dynamite in raising bodies embedded in mud were abandoned for the time being for fear the explosions might destroy any evidence the ship could give of possible mismanagement of the water ballast system, given by several marine engineers as a possible cause of the calamity.

Plans for raising the Eastland were completed today and the work will be begun as soon as the necessary machinery has been placed in position. When wrecking dredges have placed the steamer on its keel, the hull will be pumped out and a careful search made for more bodies. It will take several days to raise the steamer. Dynamite will then be used in the river to release those bodies which may be stuck in the mud. The rescue work at the steamer continued with a reduced force of divers today. F.H. Avery in charge of the divers reported to Coroner Hoffman that he believed there were about 200 bodies still in the steamer, but feared they could not be recovered until the boat is raised.

Coroner Hoffman put W.J. Wood, a naval architect, who has dubbed the Eastland "The Crank of the Lakes," in charge of all work at the wreck so that any evidence in regard to faulty construction of the ship or of improper handling might be preserved.

Repeat Charge of Negligence

The coroner, the state's attorney and city officers reiterated their charge that all possible causes for the disaster could be charged to negligence of federal inspectors, or failure of federal officers to enforce marine laws. The last inspection of the Eastland was made by Robert Reid, government inspector at St. Joseph, Mich., who found the steamer fit this spring, and procured a place as chief engineer on the boat for his son-in-law, J.M. Erickson.

Correspondence made public last night between Secretary of Commerce Redfield and William H. Hull of Benton Harbor, Mich., vice-president and general manager of the St. Joseph & Chicago Steamship Company, owner of the Eastland, in regard to the effect enforcement of the new seaman's law would have on the steamer's earnings, indicated that the department of commerce had not conceded anything that would tend to make the steamer less safe than the law demanded.

Redfield Due Today

Secretary Redfield, aroused by criticisms of his subordinates, will be in Chicago tomorrow to take charge of the government end of the investigation. He has been directed by President Wilson to do everything possible to disclose responsibility for the upsetting of the Eastland and to discover ways of preventing a repetition of such an accident....

■ ■ ■

The final death toll from the *Eastland* rested at 852.

Chicago officials had known two years before the disaster that the *Eastland* was unsound. Two naval architects had written reports stating that the ship was top-heavy. The *Eastland*'s owners had added extra decks so the ship could carry more passengers. During previous voyages crew members sometimes had to order passengers to move from one side of the ship to the other to prevent listing. An Illinois court, however, ruled that the *Eastland* was seaworthy and blamed the disaster on negligence by the ship's engineer.

The *Eastland* was eventually pulled out of the river, repaired, and given a new name. As the U.S.S. *Wilmette* the ship served as a naval training ship for a number of years.

Mont Blanc-Imo Collision

Halifax, Nova Scotia, Canada
December 6, 1917
Death Toll: 1,200–1,600 (estimated)

Halifax, the capital of Nova Scotia, was a bustling city during World War I. Its harbor could accommodate the world's largest ships, and convoys often sailed from there to Europe. On December 6, 1917, the ships gathered there included a British naval cruiser and various cargo ships, including the *Mont Blanc*. This French freighter was just entering the harbor from New York, loaded with dynamite for the war effort. Unfortunately, the Belgian ship *Imo* was leaving the harbor at the same time, leading to a collision and one of the very worst accidental explosions in world history.

December 7, 1917

Explosion of French Munitions Ship and Fires That Follow in Halifax Kill Over 2000; Thousands Injured

Worst Disaster on the Continent—French Munitions Steamship Mont Blanc Rammed by Belgian Relief Ship—Richmond District Devastated—City in Darkness—Special Trains Rushing Aid

Scores of Injured Are Dying—Electric Light and
Gas Plants Destroyed—North End of City Wiped Out—
Hundreds Killed by Falling Buildings—Property Loss
Runs Far Into Millions—Whole Blocks in Ruins

Halifax, N.S., Dec. 7.—With the toll of dead steadily mounting, it was believed early this morning that more than 2,000 persons perished in the explosion and fire which followed the collision yesterday morning in Halifax harbor between a munitions laden French ship and another vessel loaded with supplies for the Belgian relief commission.

The French munitions ship Mont Blanc blew up in Halifax harbor after a collision with the Belgian relief steamship Ioma at 9 o'clock Thursday morning. Thousands were injured and many of them will die. Following the explosion the Richmond district at the north end of the city was swept by fires. In Dartmouth on the opposite side of the harbor, the wreckage was almost complete, but the explosion damaged buildings all over the city, the business district being seriously affected.

Worst Disaster on Continent

The disaster, which has plunged the Dominion into mourning, probably will rank as the most fearful that ever occurred on the American continent. Residents of Halifax and thousands of volunteer relief workers who have come into the city have been almost dazed at the extent of the horror.

Temporary morgues have been established in many buildings, to which a steady procession of vehicles of all kinds have been carrying for hours the bodies of men, women and children. Most of them were so charred that they were unrecognizable. Thousands of persons seeking traces of relatives and friends have passed by the long, silent rows attempting by the flickering light of lamps and lanterns to identify the ones they sought.

Wounded Fill All Buildings

Virtually every building in the city which could be converted into a hospital is filled with wounded, many of them so desperately injured that there is no hope of their recovery. Scores already have died in these temporary hospitals. An ever increasing number is being taken from the completely devastated Richmond district to the relief station. An army of rescue workers is searching among the ruins for bodies and for those who have survived amidst the wreckage left by the explosion and fire.

City in Darkness

The city was in darkness tonight, except for flames from the fires still burning in the wrecked buildings in the north end. The electric light and gas plants have been virtually destroyed and the only lights available are kerosene lamps. They furnished the illumination by means of which surgeons and doctors toiled heroically throughout the night, caring for the injured.

Soldiers, sailors and police patrolled the streets tonight and upon them fell the major part of the burden of searching among the ruins for the dead and wounded. The Canadians were assisted in this work by the bluejackets from an American warship in the harbor.

The flame-swept area covers approximately two and one-half square miles. It begins at what is known as the North street bridge, extending north to Pier 8 on the Richmond water front and back to a point running parallel with Gottingen street. Nothing has been left standing in this section of the city.

Only a pile of smoldering ruins marks the spot where the great building of the American Sugar Refining Company stood. The drydock and the buildings which surrounded it were all destroyed. The Richmond School, which housed hundreds of children, was demolished and it is reported only three escaped.

Canadian officers who have seen long service in France characterize the catastrophe as "the most fearful which has befallen any city in the world...."

North End Laid Waste

Virtually all the north end of the city was laid waste and the property damage will run far into the millions. A part of the town of Dartmouth across the harbor from Halifax also was wrecked. Nearly all the buildings in the dockyard there are in ruins.

The zone of destruction in Halifax itself extends from the North street railway station as far north as Africville to Bedford Basin and covers an area of about two square miles in the section known as Richmond. The buildings that were not demolished by the force of the terrific explosion were destroyed by the fire which followed.

Scores of persons were injured by the collapse of the railway station, arena rink, military gymnasium, sugar refinery and elevator.

All Business Suspended

All business has been suspended. Armed guards of soldiers and sailors are patrolling the city. Not a street car is moving and part of Halifax is in darkness tonight. All hospitals and many private houses are filled with injured. Temporary hospitals and morgues have been opened in school houses in the western section of the city.

Havoc in Harbor

The damage along the water front cannot yet be estimated. Many of the men composing the crews of the ships in the harbor were killed and injured. On one steamer, the Picyou, it is reported that thirty-three of the crew of forty-two were killed. Bodies of many seamen have been picked up in the harbor. Rescue parties working among the ruins of buildings are removing the bodies of the dead.

Struck on Port Side

The collision, which resulted in probably the worst disaster in the history of the Dominion, occurred near Pier No. 8 in the narrows leading from the harbor to Bedford Basin. The munitions ship was bound from New York for Bedford Basin when the relief ship, bound for sea, crashed into her. The Mont Blanc was pierced on the port side almost to the engine room. The other ship, which was only slightly damaged, backed away when flames burst out on the munitions ship, and was abandoned by the crew. The captain of the Mont Blanc also ordered his crew to the boats as he realized an

explosion was inevitable. The men reached shore safely before the tremendous blast seventeen minutes later, which blew their ship to pieces and wrecked a large part of the city.

Buildings Collapse

The business life of the city had just begun for the day when the town was shaken to its foundations by the explosion. Persons in the streets were picked up bodily and hurled to the ground. Occupants of office buildings cowered under a shower of falling glass and plaster. Houses in the Richmond section crumpled up and collapsed, burying their tenants.

In the main part of the city, where the buildings are chiefly of steel or concrete, the damage was confined to the shattering of windows and most of the casualties in this section were caused by flying glass. In the west and northwest ends the damage was more extensive and there the walls of many houses were blown to atoms.

Whole Blocks in Ruins

It was in Richmond, however, opposite the scene of the explosion, that the havoc was greatest.

Whole blocks of dwellings, mostly of frame construction, were leveled. Street after street is in ruins and the structures which were left standing by the explosion were destroyed by fires which started simultaneously in a score of places and which it was impossible to check until they had burned themselves out. It is believed scores of persons who had been injured in the collapse of their homes perished in the flames from which they were helpless to flee. The fires in this district are smoldering tonight....

Seek Refuge in Fields

In less than half an hour after the disaster, 5,000 persons had gathered on the common and thousands of others had sought refuge in fields outside the city. Hundreds were reported missing by their relatives and it was not known whether they were alive or dead.

The work of rescue and relief was promptly

organized. The Academy of Music and many other public buildings were thrown open to house the homeless. Five hundred tents have been erected on the common and these will be occupied by the troops who have surrendered their barracks to the women and children.

Stream of Ambulances

Every nook and cranny in all available buildings was made ready within an hour to receive the wounded. A steady stream of ambulances and automobiles arrived at hospitals which soon were filled to capacity with the injured. Doctors, nurses and volunteers toiled ceaselessly in their work of succor. Their ranks soon were swollen by others who arrived in constantly increasing number from nearby towns. It was announced before nightfall that twenty-five of the injured had died.

Those who were only slightly injured were sent to their own homes or to those of friends after their wounds had been treated. There were hundreds of cases of serious injury, however, and it is expected the death toll will be greatly increased by those who succumb to their wounds.

Automobiles were still scurrying about all sections of the city tonight carrying blanket-clad burdens. A committee of citizens already has been formed and assistance is asked from all outside points. The supplies needed are glass, tar paper, beaver board, putty, bedding and blankets. The mayors of all towns in the province have been asked to rush supplies to Halifax.

Wires All Torn Down

The force of the explosion was felt at Truro, seventy-five miles away, where windows were shattered. All telegraph and telephone wires were torn down and for several hours Halifax was completely isolated from the outside world.

Power Plants Disabled

The concussion shattered the big gas tanks of the city. All power plants are out of commission and newspaper offices have been so badly wrecked that publication is impossible.

Pilot Frank Mackie of the Mont Blanc declared tonight that the collision resulted from a confusion of whistles sounded by the Ioma. He believes the fire which caused the explosion was due to the fact that the munitions ship carried a deck load of benzine.…

Worse Than Battle

Colonel Mackenzie Bell, who spent two years on the firing line in Flanders, said tonight he never had seen anything on the battle front to equal the scenes of destruction he witnessed in Halifax today.

Hotel Guests Safe

It was reported tonight that all the guests in the hotels of the city are safe. Some of them were cut by flying glass but none was seriously injured. Two members of the crew of the Canadian cruiser Niobe were killed by the explosion and several were injured.

Feared Air Attack

The horrors of an air raid possessed the minds of many when the explosion on the Mont Blanc shook this fortress town. There were three distinct shocks. First a comparatively light rumble like a seismic disturbance startled the city. A moment later a terrific blast made even the citadel quake. Then a crash of glass throughout a wide area completed the confusion. Thousands rushing into the open saw a thick cloud of gray smoke hanging over the north end of the city. This strengthened their conviction of an attack from the air.

It was feared that other explosions would follow and, so far as possible, the frightened ones were herded in the southern part of the city. Great crowds gathered in open lots and remained there for hours until they believed all danger was past.…

■ ■ ■

The accident occurred in a narrow channel of the harbor. The *Imo* came around a bend in the channel into the *Mont Blanc's* course. Neither ship could stop or swerve to avoid the fatal collision.

Quick thinking and luck prevented an even greater disaster. A British seaman on board another freighter carrying ammunition managed to sink the ship before its cargo caught fire and exploded. Further, the blast created a tsunami in the harbor that drenched ammunition stored at a naval facility, preventing another explosion. Finally, heavy snows helped stop the fires raging through Halifax. Still, the *Mont Blanc* explosion destroyed 2½ square miles of the city's north side.

December 9, 1917

4,000 Killed in Halifax Is Latest Official Estimate

City Ceases to Number Dead, Directing its Energies to Aid of Living—Courage of Local Authorities in Situation Commands Admiration—Organization of Relief Units Under Way—Massachusetts Relief Train Arrives

Street Cars Move; Partial Lighting

Halifax, N.S., Dec. 8.—Four thousand dead. This is the new estimate tonight of the superintendent of morgues whose duty is to assemble and expose for identification, if possible, the bodies of those who perished by shock or fire when the ammunition ship Mont Blanc blew up in the harbor Thursday.

His estimate, that startled even those who had lived through three days of the horror here, was based upon the records of his district assistants who late tonight reported a total of 1,000 bodies recovered. They have figured on a certain number for a prescribed area. There appears to be no other way of determining the loss. Hundreds, perhaps thousands of bodies have been consumed by the flames and in scores of cases not only whole families but whole neighborhoods have been wiped out and the names of all their dead may never be known.

Others think this estimate too high, but all admit that the superintendent's way of figuring is as good as any.

Late in the day, dredging parties working under the direction of naval authorities dragged ashore 200 bodies of sailors, soldiers and laborers recovered from the bottom of the harbor. Another searching squad reported having found forty bodies in the hulk of the Norwegian steamer Imo, which collided with the Mont Blanc.

The work of relief was organized today at a meeting of American and Canadian officials and volunteers who are here with generous resources at their command to restore, so far as possible, the injured and provide shelter, food and clothing for the 20,000 who are destitute.

Late tonight authorities in charge of the various morgues announced that about 400 of the 1,000 bodies had been identified.

The outstanding fact that has been faced by the local authorities with a courage that challenges the admiration of their kinsmen from south of the border, is that 20,000 persons are destitute and of the number perhaps one out of seven is suffering from injuries which in many cases are bound to prove fatal.

Tonight the work of organizing the various relief units into a workable whole with a general direction that would avoid duplication of effort and tend to the greatest efficiency was well under way. Federal, provincial and Red Cross aid, supplemented by volunteer units from other cities and the United States, were being utilized to the best advantage. The Massachusetts relief train which had been stalled much of the night in snow drifts near the Nova Scotian border arrived today, bringing the first contingent of physicians, nurses and supplies. It was the first of several trains en route from the American side.

More than a foot of snow fell last night. Today the storm passed and the weather was clear and cold. Street cars were stalled in the drifts during the night but today the service had been partially restored. The day also saw the lighting system renewed in part, and after darkness fell the city looked a little less black and forbidding.

Fortunately the telephone service is good, but there is a somber significance in the report of so many "dead" numbers.

The water supply is causing the most concern.

Emergency repairs are being made as fast as it is humanly possible, but the system was still seriously deranged this evening.

The property loss variously estimated at from $20,000,000 to $50,000,000 probably will prove to be nearer the minimum figure. The relief committees have asked for $30,000,000 which they estimate will be necessary to care for the 20,000 destitute ones....

■ ■ ■

After the explosion rumors spread that the initial collision of the *Imo* and the *Mont Blanc* was actually an act of war, and that German spies were in the area. One rumor said Canadian officials executed eight Germans in connection with the explosion; another claimed that the Germans had a secret underground radio station in Halifax. Both rumors were false.

Though the death toll from the disaster was later lowered, the *Mont Blanc* explosion also destroyed about 3,000 houses and injured more than 8,000 people. Halifax recovered from this terrible disaster, and in World War II it once again served as Canada's chief naval port.

Brooklyn Rapid Transit Subway Derailment

Brooklyn, New York
November 1, 1918
Death Toll: 102

New York City experimented with underground train lines, or subways, shortly after the Civil War, but the city didn't open its first permanent system until 1904. By that time Boston had established America's first subway line, although New York's system eventually would become the largest in the country, with 238 miles of tracks. The New York City subway system holds the world record for most stations as well, with 468.

New York also claims a more dubious distinction, as the site of the worst U.S. subway disaster ever.

November 2, 1918

100 Or More Die In Crash On B.R.T. During First Day Of Strike Called by Motormen

Car in Charge of "Green" Motorman Jumps Track and Car Behind Plunges Into It—Both Crowded With Passengers—Disaster Takes Place in Malbone Street Tunnel Near Prospect Park Station—85 Bodies Removed From Wreck

Wrecked Cars Take Fire
Probably 200 Injured

New York, Nov. 1.—Eighty-five bodies had been removed late tonight from what is known as the Malbone street "tunnel," on the Brighton Beach line of the Brooklyn Rapid Transit Company, where a five car train running at high speed jumped the track on a curve and struck the side wall with such terrific force that the first car was demolished and the others "buckled" until they were jammed against the roof of the tunnel. The train, which carried nearly 900 passengers, was in charge of a "green" motorman.

First Day of Strike

The tragedy marked the first day of a strike called by the company's motormen to enforce the reinstatement of twenty-nine discharged members of the Brotherhood of Locomotive Engineers as ordered by the rational war labor board.

Officials of the company professed, three hours after the accident, to have no definite information as to its cause. They said no reports had been made to them by members of the train crew.

Arrests Ordered

District Attorney Lewis of Kings County declared all the officials of the Brooklyn Rapid Transit Company and every person connected in any way with the accident has been ordered placed under arrest. He asserted the company was withholding the name of the motorman. It was reported, however, that the man in charge of the train formerly was employed as a train dispatcher.

Made Turn at High Speed

"There is no doubt," Mr. Lewis said, "that the motorman of the leading train was going at a high rate of speed when he made the turn into the cut. The front car jumped the track and buckled. The train following ran into the stalled car."

Green Motorman

According to survivors of the wreck, the motorman evidently was unused to the road, as he was compelled to back up at one point when he had taken the wrong switch.

Both trains were jammed with passengers, as the strike had resulted in a material reduction in service and consequent delay.

Wrecked Cars Take Fire

Immediately after the crash, the wrecked cars burst into flame, adding to the terror of those who had escaped injury and increasing the peril of those pinned in the wreckage.

Police reserves from a dozen stations were rushed to the scene of the accident and they immediately sent in calls for all the ambulances in Brooklyn, while Manhattan hospitals were asked for assistance. The fire department also was called upon to aid the injured and remove the dead.

Rescue Work Slow

Rescue work was retarded by the fact that the crash occurred in a deep cut. It was rather difficult for relief workers or survivors to clamber up and down the steep concrete walls of what is known as the Malbone street "tunnel."

Carried Up Ladders

The injured and dead were carried up ladders taken from fire apparatus. Charred bodies were placed in burlap bags to shroud them from the gaze of the thousands of persons who gathered within a few minutes after the collision. Policemen and firemen were literally mobbed by frenzied men and women who feared the burdens they carried might be members of their families.

Hundreds of reserves formed a cordon around the "tunnel" and kept back the great throng from the long line of ambulances which came clanging from every direction. More than 100 members of the women's motor corps of America responded with their cars to the calls for help. All kinds of vehicles were pressed into service to carry the dead and injured to hospitals and morgues.

Trains Packed

The trains were packed with workers in Manhattan and with shoppers who had been detained on the New York side of the river by the crush in the Brooklyn bridge station resulting from the reduced train service. Many of those on board were children.

Survivors Panic-Stricken

Survivors of the crash crawled from the wreckage and ran through the tunnel, screaming and weeping, unmindful of the danger from the live third rails which bordered the tracks. Their cries quickly brought aid from persons living in the neighborhood, who gave what assistance they could until police and firemen arrived.

According to the passengers it became evident soon after the train left Brooklyn bridge that the motorman was unfamiliar with the line which runs on the elevated structure until it reaches Franklin avenue, where it descends gradually to the surface and enters the cut.

Failed to Slacken Speed

When the train reached the "tunnel," passengers told the police, the motorman failed to slacken speed as he should have done. Suddenly, the first car left the track and plunged into the concrete wall, dragging the cars behind with it....

Horrible Scenes

The rescuers who arrived at the scene of the wreck first found women and girls with their arms around each other caught beneath seats that were torn and broken and partly burned. In the first car passengers were pinned against the roof and against the walls. Some had been pierced with splinters of wood, while others had been mortally wounded by the broken glass. Even the police and firemen were aghast at the carnage they came upon in the heart of the wreckage, under tons of debris. Almost every body there was mutilated beyond recognition.…

Cars All of Wood

The cars in the wrecked train were all of wood. The public service commission ordered the B.R.T. many months ago to replace the wooden rolling stock with steel, but the company contended it was impossible, because of war conditions, to obtain the new cars, and it was given permission to use those on hand until its orders were filled by the manufacturers.

District Attorney Lewis, late tonight, made the following formal statement regarding the wreck:—

"After a thorough and minute investigation of this accident—the worst and most terrible traction accident that ever happened in Brooklyn—I have come to the conclusion that it was due to the recklessness of the motorman, William Lewis. The man was incompetent. He had no right to be running this train. His incompetence must have been known to the officials of the Brooklyn Rapid Transit Company."

President Williams of the B.R.T. denied, late tonight, that the motorman in charge of the train was a "green" hand. He declared he was a motor switchman whose duty it had been to run trains in and out of yards, and that he must, of necessity, have been familiar with their operation.

■ ■ ■

November 3, 1918

Mayor Hylan in Charge of B.R.T. Wreck Inquiry

Presides as Committing Magistrate and Issues Two Warrants Charging Manslaughter

New York, Nov. 2.—Two investigations were started today of the wreck which occurred last night in the Malbone street tunnel of the Brooklyn Rapid Transit Company when a heavily laden Brighton Beach train, said to have been operated by a "green" motorman, leaped a curve, killing eighty-nine persons and injuring nearly double that number.

One investigation was started by Mayor Hylan and Harry E. Lewis, district attorney of King's County, to fix the blame for the accident and to present evidence to the November grand jury which Mr. Lewis announced he would summon Monday.

A supplementary investigation was begun by the public service commission which announced tonight that it would turn over the reports of its experts to District Attorney Lewis.

For perhaps the first time in the history of this city its chief executive has presided as committing magistrate. Mayor Hylan today opened the "John Doe" inquiry started by District Attorney Lewis after the mayor had asked for prosecution of Brooklyn Rapid Transit officials, whom he blamed for the wreck because they failed to reinstate twenty-nine men, as recommended by the war labor board. Failure of the company, he contended, led to the strike, settled early this morning, and to the utilization of inexperienced motormen.

One of the mayor's first acts as presiding magistrate was to issue two warrants, charging manslaughter in the second degree, for "John Doe" and "Richard Roe." The investigation at which the mayor is presiding is scheduled to continue Monday, when it is expected that the real names of the persons for whom the warrants have been issued will be made known.

Mayor Visits Injured

Before the investigation was started, the mayor visited many of the injured in hospitals, questioning them and telling them that every effort would be made "to see that the guilty are punished." Virtually all the survivors interviewed by the mayor declared that the train was going "very fast" when the crash came, a statement that was corroborated by William Lewis, the motorman who operated the train on its fatal trip, after he had been arrested on a charge of homicide and questioned by District Attorney Lewis. With Lewis were arrested Sam Rossof and Michael Turner, conductor and guard, respectively, on the train.

According to Lewis, the train of five cars, three of which were antiquated wooden coaches, was traveling at thirty miles an hour when it entered the tunnel. He declared that he tried to apply the brakes to slow down the train to six miles an hour, the speed called for in entering the tunnel. According to Lewis, the brakes "didn't seem to work."

Lewis and Rossof were held without bail after they had pleaded not guilty to the charges against them. Turner wasn't arraigned because of injuries which confined him to a hospital.…

■ ■ ■

One of the men charged with manslaughter was William Lewis, the motorman (driver) of the subway. Lewis had suffered a string of bad luck before the crash: he had been sick with the flu, his baby had died just weeks before, and he was exhausted from working overtime on the subway. His failure to slow down the train, plus the defective brakes, led to the fatal accident. However, Lewis was found not guilty of manslaughter.

A total of 97 passengers died at the scene of the crash, and five more died later from their injuries. Less than two months after the accident, the Brooklyn Rapid Transit Company went bankrupt.

Explosion of the *Hindenburg*

Lakehurst, New Jersey
May 6, 1937
Death Toll: 36

Like the first airplanes, dirigibles proved useful during World War I. One new type of dirigible flown during the war was called a *rigid airship*. This craft featured a metal frame surrounding a series of bags that were filled with gas. After the war rigid airships were used commercially to carry passengers and became the "ocean liners of the sky."

The 1920s and 1930s were the golden age of dirigibles. Within the gondola of a rigid airship passengers slept in comfortable cabins and socialized in public rooms. Dirigibles made the transatlantic crossing in about three days—faster than a ship. For the wealthy, dirigibles were a unique traveling experience.

But dirigibles were also dangerous. Hydrogen—a gas often used to raise the craft off the ground—is extremely flammable. Even when the safer gas helium was used, dirigibles were vulnerable to bad weather and fires on board. Almost all the major aviation disasters of the era involved these airships.

To the passengers of the *Hindenburg* any risk was worth the adventure of flying on the largest airship ever built. The *Hindenburg* was 804 feet long and could carry its 97 passengers and 61 crew members at speeds up to 85 miles per hour. Unfortunately, the German dirigible was held aloft by hydrogen, which led to the grand airship's fiery end.

May 7, 1937

35 to 40 Killed When Giant Air Liner 'Hindenburg' Plunges To Earth In Flames

Explosion Destroys Big German Zeppelin At Lakehurst Airport

20 Passengers, 44 Crew Survive

Estimates of Death Toll Conflicting; Spark of Static Electricity or Backfiring of Engine Among Theories as to Cause of Disaster; Captain Pruss and Captain Lehmann, His Adviser, Among Saved; Some Injured in Hospitals Not Expected to Live; Spectators Describe Horror

Lakehurst, N.J., May 6.—(AP.)—Her silvery bulk shattered by a terrific explosion, the German airliner "Hindenburg" plunged in flames at the United States Naval Air Station tonight, with indications at least one-third of the 99 aboard perished.

As minor explosions continued to tear her twisted aluminum skeleton and ribboned fabric hours afterward, estimates of the death toll were conflicting and duplicating.

Figures Conflicting

Harry A. Bruno, press relations counsel for the Zeppelin company, which operated the luxurious modern dirigible, said that 64 of the persons aboard her on her first 1937 voyage here had been reported saved. He listed 20 passengers and 44 of the crew as survivors.

Captains Escape

Official sources listed among the survivors the new commander of the big ship, Captain Max Pruss, and the veteran skipper, Captain Ernst Lehmann, who commanded it on 10 trips between the United States and Germany last year. Another of the crew, a Captain Stampf, also was listed as a survivor.

Timothy W. Margerum of Lakewood said there were already 40 bodies in the naval station's garage which had been hurriedly transformed into a morgue. Many of the dead were horribly burned by the oil-fed flames. Margerum reported others were dying. Hospitals for miles around were filled with the injured.

The Navy Department in Washington said it was advised at least 48 persons were killed.

Blast In No. 2 Cell

An explosion of the No. 2 gas cell toward the stern of the ship was named as the cause of the disaster by State Aviation Commissioner Gill Robb Wilson, who called the blast "strange." The highly-inflammable hydrogen gas billowed into fierce flame as the explosion plummeted the ship to the airfield. Ground spectators said crew members in the stern of the ship "never had a chance to escape."

No Warning

The disaster struck without the least warning. The ship had angled her blunt nose toward the mooring mast, the spider-like landing lines had been snaked down from her belly and the ground crew had grasped the ropes from the nose, when the explosion roared out, scattering ground crew and spectators like frightened sheep.

The passengers, who were waving gaily a minute before, from the observation windows that slit the belly of the dirigible, were so stunned they could not describe later what happened. Some jumped to the sandy landing field along with members of the crew. Others seemed to have been pitched from the careening sky liner as it made its death plunge.

As flames engulf the Hindenburg, *the airship crashes to the ground at the U.S. Naval Air Station in Lakehurst, New Jersey, on May 6, 1937.*

Rescuers Driven Back

The heat drove back would-be rescuers, so it could not be determined for how many the "Hindenburg" made a burning tomb. Fire departments from nearby communities converged on the field and soon had streams of water playing on the broken airliner. The flames still enveloped the outline of the ship, apparently feeding on the fuel oil supply which the "Hindenburg" carried for her Diesel motors.

Somewhere in the glowing furnace were the two dogs, 340 pounds of mail and the ton of baggage which she had aboard.

31 In Hospitals

Thirty-one survivors were accounted for in hospitals and other places in the Lakehurst area at 10:45 p.m. (EDT).

F.W. von Meister, vice-president of the American Zeppelin Transport Company, the general United States agents for the German Zeppelin Transport Company, the "Hindenburg's" owners, said there were two possible causes for the explosions.

Two Theories As to Cause

First he listed the rainy condition which prevailed at the naval air station when the landing was attempted. The ship cruised around over the field for an hour to ride out a rainstorm and nosed down while rain was still falling.

The rainy condition, von Meister said, would make for the creation of a spark of static electricity when the landing ropes were dropped and such a spark might have touched off the highly explosive hydrogen gas which gave the long silver ship its lifting power.

Possibly Spark from Engine

The second theory von Meister advanced was that a spark flew from one of the engines when they were throttled down for the landing. The ship had been valving hydrogen preparatory to landing, and he theorized some of the gas might have gathered in a pocket under the tail surfaces and detonated when the spark flew back.

Some authorities scouted the theory that the explosion could have been caused by the ignition of hydrogen inside the gas cells. They said a mixture of 20 per cent free air with hydrogen would be necessary to cause an explosion, indicating the first blast must have occurred outside one of the gas cells.

Aeronautical experts said the only way they could explain an explosion inside the ship would be that free hydrogen had in some way escaped and was lying in the stern of the ship where it was accidentally ignited.

The ship was 76 hours and 23 minutes out of Frankfort-on-Main, her home port, when the disaster occurred.

Static Theory Supported

Some support of the static electricity theory was given by Major George F. Hobson of Camp Dix, who was on the field, superintending the work of soldiers working with the sailors in the ground crew.

The ground crew, he said, had hold of the spider landing ropes from the ship's nose, easing her down when there appeared to be a sudden spark near her tail fins and in an instant a third of the ship was engulfed in flames.

The ground crew, he said, dropped the landing ropes in panic-haste and raced from under the plunging, flaming ship for safety. Women fainted, men screamed as the crowd recoiled in a terrific backward surge.

A few minutes before the passengers had lined the sloping observation windows of the dirigible, waving and shouting remarks to those on the ground. Their cries rang out as the ship plunged from its low altitude.

The ground crew of sailors, which had been standing by to help land the ship, scattered before the blinding flare of the explosion. Even after the first stunning explosion sent the ship crashing, additional blasts continued to rend the "Hindenburg's" silvery bulk. Spectators sobbed hysterically at the abrupt disaster in which the "Hindenburg" had ended her first 1937 trip to America. Eighteen trips had been planned this year.

Army trucks and ambulances rushed to the tangled, burning wreck to succor those who had escaped with their lives. The body of one woman, presumably a passenger, was picked up from the landing field.

Those on the ship who survived were so stunned by the unexpected disaster they could not tell what had happened. "There was a blinding flash," said one passenger, Herbert O'Laughlin of Chicago, "but the people on the ground would know more about it than we would on the ship...."

Two Explosions

Authorities said there were two explosions in the air, followed by several lesser ones after the stricken ship settled on the ground. The lesser explosions were believed due to detonating fuel tanks. The blasts ripped the ship as if she were made of paper.

The first two blasts sent flames shooting high into the evening sky, but men standing under the ship reported they felt virtually no concussion. The explosion's force, however, was felt a little further away from the ship, those in the ring of spectators said.

Captain Ernst Lehmann, who piloted the ship on most of its trips a year ago, tottered dazedly from the wreckage and staggered toward an ambulance....

Agonizing Cries

The screams and cries of injured in agony were "terrible," the sailors and marines who did rescue work reported. The clothing was completely burned off one man. Another, blown through the envelope, was found moaning near the smashed airship.

The survivors and rescue workers told of the terrific heat which followed the explosion and the surge of fire.

Some of the spectators and ground crew men said they saw figures, apparently members of the crew, leap from the control car as it neared the ground. When the stern settled it yielded badly burned bodies, for there the fire was the worst at first.

■ ■ ■

Ferdinand von Zeppelin had perfected the rigid airship, which was sometimes called the *zeppelin* in his honor. In the 1930s the government of Nazi Germany, led by Adolf Hitler, was proud of the dirigible's German heritage and the country's engineering accomplishments with the *Hindenburg*. The explosion on the aircraft startled the Germans, and along with the rest of the world they waited to learn more about the disaster.

Navy Summons Witnesses Of Hindenburg Explosion; No Evidence Of Sabotage

Probes Ruins and Prepares for Hearings

Senate Investigator Finds No Trace of Plot But Copeland Insists It Is a Possibility

Lakehurst, N.J., May 8.—(AP)—Members of a naval board of inquiry prowled today through the junk heap that was once the dirigible Hindenburg.

They sought an answer to the baffling question of why the German Zeppelin burst into flames and crashed 1,000 feet from the end of its transatlantic voyage, bringing death to 34 of those aboard and one member of the ground crew preparing to land it at the U.S. Navy air station here.

No Trace of Sabotage

In Washington Chairman Copeland announced today that an investigator from his Senate commerce committee sent to the scene of the Hindenburg disaster had uncovered no evidence of sabotage.

Copeland added, however:

"I cannot disabuse my mind of the possibility of sabotage. I don't say that was the cause and it's purest conjecture when I suggest it, but nothing has turned up to remove sabotage as a possible cause."

The committee investigator, Col. Harold E. Hartney, gave a preliminary report to Copeland by telephone. He said he would investigate further tomorrow.

Deaths Are Now 35

The Hindenburg death total mounted to 35 when two men, Capt. William Speck of the crew and Erich Knocher, an importer, succumbed to injuries early today. Thirty-one persons remained in hospitals, two of them in serious condition.

With Capt. Gordon W. Haines as presiding

officer, the three-man board began this afternoon an investigation of all the circumstances surrounding the disaster.

Captain Haines said the inquiry would parallel one ordered by Secretary of Commerce Roper. Public hearings in both will start at the air station Monday. A third inquest, to look into the death of Allen Hagaman, a civilian ground crew member, was ordered by the station's commanding officer, Commander Charles E. Rosenthal.

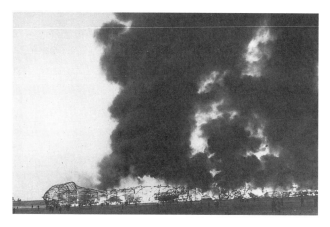

The steel frame of the Hindenburg *burns after the German airship exploded.*

Lakehurst Closed Indefinitely

Officers announced the reservation would be closed indefinitely. Regular army troops and marines from other posts doubled the usual personnel of 400 to handle 24-hour-a-day patrol duty.

The crumpled, blackened duralumin which once formed the framework of the great skyliner lay in full view of the administration building where the naval board convenes.…

Grizzled Dr. Hugo Eckener, veteran dirigible skipper and designer, headed a commission leaving Germany to come here for an investigation of the Hindenburg disaster. Pending final word on the crash, he said, the Graf Zeppelin would be grounded.…

■ ■ ■

The *Hindenburg* was not history's deadliest dirigible disaster—73 people died when the U.S. Navy airship *Akron* crashed off the coast of New Jersey in 1933—but the *Hindenburg*'s end was more spectacular and better docu-mented. The crash was even broadcast live on radio. A Chicago radio announcer, Herbert Morrison, covered the event as it happened, struggling to find words as he described the terrible flames and loss of life: "It is burning, bursting into flames and is falling…oh!…this is one of the worst…oh! It's a terrific sight…oh!…and all the humanity…"

The *Hindenburg* disaster, and the introduction of improved long-range airplanes, ended the era of transatlantic dirigible travel. Decades after the accident aviation experts still debate what caused the explosion. A newer theory says that the airship's fabric covering—not its hydrogen fuel—caught fire first, probably from a static spark.

Explosion of the *Kiangya*

Wangpoo River, China
December 3, 1948
Death Toll: 2,750

During World War II most of China was controlled by Japan. When the war ended, the Japanese gave back the territory they had seized, but fighting continued in China. The country's Communists, led by Mao Zedong, waged a rebellion against the government. By the end of 1948 the Communists had control of many major cities and were closing in on the port of Shanghai. People opposed to the Communists fled, using any transportation they could find.

When the *Kiangya,* an aging coastal steamer, pulled out of Shanghai, the ship was filled with refugees hoping to escape the advancing Communists. Their voyage was a short one.

December 5, 1948

3200 Chinese Believed Lost In Ship Blast

Cause of Disaster on Yangtze Is Unknown; Victims War Refugees

Shanghai, Dec. 4.—(AP.)—More than 3200 Chinese were estimated dead or missing tonight in the explosion of an overcrowded refugee ship in the Yangtze estuary.

Lack of passenger records made possible only the roughest figures. The exact toll never will be known.

Even approximate accuracy, however, ranks the disaster as the greatest in modern maritime history, including single-ship casualties of major wars.

Estimates of those rescued ranged from a low of 100 to a high of 700.

The 2099-ton steamer Kiangya sailed from Shanghai Friday for Ninghsien (Ningpo), 200 miles down the coast. It exploded about 10 p.m. Friday and sank within an hour, all available survivors agreed. Cause of the explosion was not known. Guesses ranged from Communist sabotage to a floating mine or possibly overtaxed boilers.

Funnel Sighted

The loss was not discovered until Saturday morning, when a passing coastal ship sighted the funnel and a bit of wrecked superstructure protruding above the shallow water.

Six Chinese tugs and former landing craft still searched the scene 30 miles northeast of Shanghai tonight.

It was considered unlikely that they would find additional survivors after more than 24 hours in the chill, wind-lashed waters.

Officials of the China Merchant Steam Navigation Company which operated the ship said its top capacity was supposed to be 1186 persons.

They estimated that actually it had carried as many as 4250, half of whom had boarded without tickets.

This was admittedly only a guess, but officials said on many recent trips since the Communist invasion scare began, more than 4000 persons had clambered aboard.

They conservatively estimated 3000 missing plus 200 bodies recovered.

No non-Chinese were known to have been aboard.

The steamship office had to close during the day as thousands of relatives of passengers sought admittance. Extra police sought vainly tonight to break up the milling horde that jammed traffic in nearby streets.

■ ■ ■

The news of the *Kiangya* led to unofficial reports of another maritime disaster. Details about an explosion on a Chinese troop transport are still sketchy today; most sources have less information than the following Associated Press item.

December 6, 1948

Second Ship Loss Bared; 6000 Perish

Chinese Sources Say Army Transport Sunk Early in November

Shanghai, Dec. 5.—(AP.)—Two Chinese ship explosions one month apart were estimated today to have taken possibly 9200 lives.

Explosion of the crowded refugee steamer Kiangya near Shanghai Friday night with loss of an estimated 3200 or more lives brought the disclosure from official Nanking sources that as many as 6000 died in a similar sinking off southern Manchuria early in November.

This larger disaster, rating as probably the greatest single-ship tragedy of modern times, was said to have involved an unidentified merchant ship which was evacuating elements of the government's 52d Army from Yingkow.

It was not announced by the military, but the sources that trickled into Nanking said the boiler burst, setting off ammunition and killing all on board.

The Yingkow evacuation fleet was under Communist artillery fire at the time, but it was not known whether this had anything to do with the explosion. No other details were obtainable.

Mine Blamed in Latest Sinking

Meanwhile, belief grew in maritime circles that a drifting World War II mine sank the refugee ship

Kiangya in the Yangtze estuary Friday night. Earlier rumors had blamed Communist sabotage.

The 2099-ton ship, jammed with Chinese seeking to escape the Communist threat to Shanghai, blew up and sank Friday night in the Yangtze River estuary.

A diver inspected the shattered hull at low tide today. He reported the entire stern was blown off. He said the wreckage was too extensive to have been caused by a saboteur's time bomb or even an exploding boiler.

The diver removed 20 bodies from below decks but had to quit when the tide rose.

About 200 bodies have been recovered.

Shen Chung-yi, vice-minister of the China Merchants Steam Navigation Company which operated the ship, said about 1000 persons had been rescued.

The little ship, bound for Ninghsien, 200 miles down the coast from Shanghai, had about 200 crew members, 2600 paying passengers, and well over 1000 who had gotten aboard without paying.

Absence of any records made it impossible ever to determine how many actually died.

Victims Swept to Sea

Survivors said, however, that hundreds were blown overboard and swept out to sea, so their bodies never will be recovered.

Rescue figures also were inaccurate because many survivors were landed at the nearest coastal point without a check.

Families of both victims and survivors continued to demonstrate noisily in front of the steamship office.

Some shouted that rescue boats had spent their time fishing luggage off the protruding superstructure rather than hunting for survivors.

■ ■ ■

The *Kiangya* did indeed hit a Japanese mine left over from World War II, and the overcrowding caused by the people frantic to escape another war added to the death toll. The *Kiangya* explosion was the one of the worst steamship disasters ever.

Three-Way Train Collision

Harrow, England
October 8, 1952
Death Toll: 112

Great Britain's worst railway disaster took place in 1915, at Gretna Junction in Scotland, when 227 people died in a four-train collision. The accident occurred during wartime, and many of the victims were soldiers on their way to fight in France, so the disaster received little news coverage at the time. Almost 40 years later Britain's next major railway disaster involved a huge three-way collision. This time the news reports were more detailed.

October 9, 1952

British Train Wreck Toll May Hit 125

85 Known Dead, 170 Hurt as 2 Expresses Rip Into Waiting Cars

HARROW, England, Oct. 8. (AP)—Two speeding express trains crashed into a crowded commuters' train within a few seconds at Harrow station today and killed at least 85 persons in a great cauldron of wreckage and hissing steam. Forty more may be found under the mass of debris.

The known toll of injured taken to hospitals was 170.

Late tonight, 16 hours after the wreck, rescuers still were digging into a 55-foot high mound of wreckage toward a coach buried at the bottom of the heap. Searchers figured probably 40 were entombed in the coach.

Scotland Yard at one time tonight announced the death figure at 116, but later said this was an error.

Becomes Human Jack

Under the glare of arc lights, workmen pumped oxygen into the mangled debris in Harrow station while searchers with acetylene torches burned away entombing steel beams.

Policeman John McIntyre turned himself into a human jack to rescue three trapped women. He crawled into the debris and heaved up the broken side of a coach with his shoulders while others pulled out the women one by one.

Harrow station looked as though it had been blitzed.

Officials said the death toll might climb above 120 in this worst British railway disaster since 227 persons were killed and 246 injured in a collision of two passengers trains and a troop train at Gratna, Scotland, May 15, 1915.

Platform Standees Mowed Down

The tremendous impact hurled two big locomotives across the jam-packed station platform, mowing down scores of waiting passengers.

The wreckage erupted into a mound 55 feet high which tore away large sections of an overhead footpath and spilled pedestrians into the cauldron below.

Rescue workers, many of them veterans of wartime air raids, were still digging in the wreckage for survivors and dead eight hours after the crash. Some tore at the twisted, telescoped coaches with their bare hands.

The wreck came at the height of the morning rush hour.

A local train from Tring to London, 11 miles from Harrow, was waiting on Platform 4. Crowds of commuters steadily boarded it. Nearby, men and women waited, chatting or reading newspapers.

Suddenly there was a shriek of the Perth-London express train, running 95 minutes late.

The speeding express crashed into the rear of the waiting local with a grinding, crunching roar, spilling wreckage across an adjoining track.

Moments later, the express from London to Manchester, coming from the opposite direction, barreled into the wreckage.

Coaches smashed into other coaches, slivers of wood and metal sprayed over a wide area. Flying glass sang through the air like shrapnel.

Within seconds the station looked as if it had been hit in an air raid. Flying debris stopped the station clock at 8:19 a.m.

Pitiful reminders of what had started as routine commuting trips and holiday journeys lay scattered hundreds of yards from the torn and ripped tracks.

Here lay a woman's brown high heeled shoe. Here a hat. There a ripped jacket. A child's shoe, caught by its laces, dangled from a razor-edged piece of metal.

Wreckage from the three trains covers the tracks in Harrow, England, after the fatal collision at the train station there on October 8, 1952.

Screams Puncture Silence

From the mangled coaches came the occasional screams of the injured—but mostly there was the silence of death.

A number of school children were believed among the dead.

A U.S. serviceman was on the first death list issued by the state-owned British railways. His name was given as Donald G. Woodvale of the U.S. Air Force. His rank and home town were not stated.

Anthony V. Gregory, a portrait photographer who lives near the station, said:

"What struck me immediately was how oddly quiet it was. There was a hiss of escaping steam and low moans from people trapped in the cars. But there were few outcries.

"Soon the only sound you were aware of was the creak of ambulances arriving in relays to take away the injured and the chopping of firemen, policemen and rail workers working quickly to free people trapped in the cars."

Scores of U.S. Air Force men from nearby bases administered blood plasma and gave transfusions. Harrow railway officials estimated the American first aid teams saved at least 20 lives.

The rescue work began in a matter of minutes after the crash.

There were about 1,000 persons aboard the three trains. About a dozen coaches were smashed in the wreck. All the locomotives involved were steam engines.

The exact cause of the disaster was still undetermined.

■ ■ ■

October 10, 1952

Train Crash Toll Is Revised to 99

HARROW, Eng., Oct. 9—(AP) Dirt-streaked rescuers lifted off another layer of wreckage from Harrow's triple train collision tonight and found five more dead, bringing the toll to 99.

Earlier, 14 bodies were pulled from the bottom of the ruins of two coaches of a packed commuters' local which were flattened yesterday when two express trains from opposite directions thundered into them seconds apart.

The day after the three-way collision, a crane lifts one of the damaged locomotives off the track. Smashed cars are stacked up on the right.

J.W. Watkins, regional controller of the British railways, told newsmen the rescuers were about finished searching the ruins. "There may be one or two more or some scattered limbs, but we're just about through," he said.

But anguished relatives from all parts of England still waited for word from some of the 1,000 passengers who were on the three trains.

Hospitals still held 94 injured after discharging 63.

At least three Americans were believed among the dead.…

The cause of the wreck still was undetermined. A government investigation into Britain's worst train disaster in 37 years has been set for next Wednesday.

■ ■ ■

A board of inquiry determined that the engineer on the express train traveling from Perth to London had missed or ignored a signal warning that the local train was stopped on the tracks ahead. The engineer was one of the 112 victims of the crash.

Capsizing of the *Toya Maru*

**Hakodate, Japan
September 26, 1954
Death Toll: 1,172**

Typhoons and hurricanes have plagued sailors for centuries, overturning ships or wiping out entire fleets (see Volume 4, *Tornadoes and Cyclones*). Even modern steel ships are not safe from the ravages of a killer storm, as the passengers on the Japanese ferry *Toya Maru* learned.

September 27, 1954

Japanese Ferry Capsizes 1,000 Are Feared Drowned

TOKYO, Monday, Sept. 27 (AP)—Nearly 1,000 persons, including 53 Americans, were missing and presumed drowned today after a huge ferry capsized last night in the typhoon-lashed seas off the northern Japanese island of Hokkaido.

The U.S. Far East Command reported at least 12 American military personnel of 52 aboard the 4,337-ton ferry Toya Maru were known to have perished. The other American was Thomas M. West, 60, an agent for a cosmetic firm.

They were among 1,141 passengers on the southbound vessel when mammoth waves flipped it on its side in Hakodate Harbor.

442 Bodies Recovered

The Japanese Maritime Safety Board reported there were 155 survivors, but did not say whether any Americans were among them. The board said 442 bodies had been recovered and 544 persons still were missing.…

The joint staff council, Japan's top military headquarters, described the disaster as the worst in Japan's maritime history.

400 Bodies Washed Ashore

Japan's Maritime Safety Board reported 400 bodies were washed ashore and 42 were aboard the ship, possibly crushed when railroad cars aboard broke loose and plunged across the decks.

All, or almost all, the other Americans were servicemen or their dependents.

The death toll may be heavily swelled by other ship disasters.

The typhoon, third to lash Japan within two weeks, also fanned a fierce fire which destroyed four-fifths of the coastal city of Iwanai on western Hokkaido. Iwanai has a population of 23,000.

Communications were tangled in the area, but the death toll was expected to mount when details of the fire are learned.…

The Toya Maru had just left Hakodate at 6:30 p.m., bound south for Aomori on Honshu, the main Japanese island. Several such big ferries, which carry whole trains, are the main link between Honshu and the northern island of Hokkaido across Tsugaru Strait. The Toya Maru recently carried Emperor Hirohito and Empress Nagako on their trip to Hokkaido in August. The typhoon hit Japan's southern island of Kyushu at 1 a.m. Sunday, raked most of the island empire, including Tokyo, and then crossed westward into the Japan Sea.

Then, suddenly, it cut back just in time to lash Tsugaru Strait with the full fury of 110-mile winds, piling water up in giant waves in Hokkaido's funnel-like bays.

The Toya Maru carried some 40 railway cars which shifted while the ferry was trying to find shelter outside Hakodate Harbor. The shift abruptly plunged the hundreds of passengers into giant waves whipped up by the storm. Few had any chance of rescue.

Small boats patrol the waters around the ferry Toya Maru, still looking for victims more than a week after the ship capsized near Hakodate, Japan, in 1954.

Anchor Chain Breaks

The ferry carried 1,127 passengers. Just before it upset, the ferry had tried to unload passengers onto lighters. Breaking of an anchor chain halted that move. It then moved toward shore but the shift of the railway cars dumped the passengers before the craft could be beached. The U.S. 1st Cavalry Division had been stationed on Hokkaido for several years and just recently completed moving its unit south to Honshu.

Crippled communications yielded only the most meager details.

Kyodo news service gave this sketchy account on the ferry tragedy:

The 4,300-ton Toya Maru, which plies between northernmost Hokkaido and the main island of Honshu, was carrying 1,127 passengers, including 56 foreigners, and some 40 rail coaches.

Ferry Took Shelter

On its 150-mile run, the ferry took shelter outside Hakodate Harbor.

The rail coaches slipped to one side and the ferry overturned. Huge wind-churned waves then battered it.

Asahi said 200 bodies were recovered. Radio station NHK, which has radio contact with Hokkaido, said only 40 persons from the ferry were definitely known to have made safely to shore.

An American LST (landing ship-tank) No. 546 was grounded intentionally on Hokkaido to save its load of American troops from the wild sea, Maritime Safety Board headquarters informed The Associated Press.

It was not known immediately how many troops were aboard the 2,700-ton craft.

Prior to the Hokkaido fatalities, Japanese police had reported to Asahi that the typhoon's toll on islands to the south yesterday was: 43 dead, 82 missing, 371 injured, 1,572 houses destroyed, 511 boats and ships sunk and many other houses and ships damaged.

The typhoon had swept through south Japan Saturday and Sunday, then moved north over the Sea of Japan. It had slammed into the southern area from the Pacific swiftly, causing widespread destruction although only brushing Tokyo.

When it passed Honshu Island, the typhoon was believed to be harmlessly dissipating. But it swung in toward Hokkaido and dealt a devastating blow Sunday night.

Because forecasters said this typhoon, the 15th of the year, was not as strong as earlier ones, the precautions taken had not been so extensive.

Two typhoons earlier this month killed 93.

■ ■ ■

September 28, 1954

Typhoon Toll May Hit 1,600; 50 Yanks Are Still Missing

HAKODATE, Japan, Tuesday, Sept. 28 (AP)—Bodies and debris strewed the beaches here today after a savage typhoon sank a huge ferry and killed possibly 1,600 persons in Northern Japan.

Seventeen Americans—soldiers, their dependents and civilians—were among the dead. Nearly 50 other Americans were listed as missing by the U.S. Army and Japan National Railway.

The Americans died in Japan's worst maritime disaster Sunday when the typhoon, which had been heading out across the Sea of Japan, turned and struck Northern Japan with winds of 100 m.p.h.

The Toya Maru with an estimated 1,200 persons aboard had anchored off Hakodate harbor when the rush of wind and water hit. It capsized. Only 163 persons were known to have survived.

Four other ferries from Hakodate were also caught and sank. The tides still were washing in bodies. Rescue workers searched the beaches and debris in the hope of finding more alive.

The Marine Safety Board said that throughout the storm area, 12 steamships, 25 motor schooners and 312 other vessels sank. It listed 1,552 persons dead or missing from sea disasters alone.

The board's figures cover an area from Southern Japan, where the typhoon first struck, to North Japan. It said never before in history had a typhoon wrought such damage in the seas around Japan.

Two U.S. Navy ships and planes from four U.S. bases in Japan launched a survivor search but stiff winds and high waves kept rescue work at a minimum.

The typhoon's winds whipped up a great fire that within minutes destroyed 3,000 to 4,300 houses at Iwanai, a city of 23,000 population 90 miles north of Hakodate. Police said 32 were dead there and 56 missing.

Police and coast guard estimated 600 bodies had washed ashore by Monday night. About 500 bodies were believed caught in the hull of the Toya Maru, which sank only 150 yards from the shore.

Some bodies probably came from the four other ferries, which carried about 300 crewmen. Police said only about 45 were known to have survived from the sinking of the four.

All Reported Safe

A U.S. tank landing ship, carrying 191 soldiers of the U.S. 1st Cavalry Division, ran aground during the big blow but all aboard were reported safe.

About 60 Japanese were killed, police estimated, by the typhoon Sunday when it roared across the main islands of Kyushu and Honshu. It then moved on north into the Sea of Japan.

Instead of heading for Siberia, as expected, the typhoon began generating 100-mile winds. It then turned and struck the Tsugaru Strait, which separates the northern island of Hokkaido from the main home island of Honshu.

The Toya Maru had set out from Hakodate for Aomori, on the northern shore of Honshu. With the hoisting of storm warnings, it anchored outside the harbor.

When the great seas swept in, the anchor chain broke, engines went dead and several dozen railway cars in the hold apparently broke loose, causing the ferry to capsize.

■ ■ ■

Andrea Doria-Stockholm Collision

**Off the Coast of Massachusetts
July 25, 1956
Death Toll: 51**

During World War II many ocean liners were converted into troop transports, ferrying soldiers and supplies around the world. In one wartime accident the French liner *Normandie* burned in New York Harbor as the U.S. government prepared it for naval service. In an even greater disaster the *Queen Mary,* an 81,000-ton liner, collided with a British cruiser, splitting the warship in two and killing more than 300 sailors. Soon after the war, however, luxurious ocean cruising returned to the Atlantic.

With a rich sailing heritage, Italy was proud of its new ocean liners, which included the *Andrea Doria.* Like all ships built after 1948, the Italian liner was equipped with radar— a wartime invention of the British with many applications for peacetime transportation—but even that safety device didn't prevent a disaster at sea.

July 27, 1956

Greatest Sea Rescue In History Marks Sinking Of Andrea Doria

Most Of 1,709 Aboard Italian Ship Saved

8 Die, Many Hurt, 50 Missing In Collision; Stockholm Limps

NEW YORK, July 26 (AP)—Italy's pride of the seas, the 30,000-ton luxury liner Andrea Doria, sank today in the Atlantic after an unexplained collision with the Swedish liner Stockholm. A Herculean rescue operation saved most of the 1,709 persons aboard the Italian vessel.

There were 8 known dead and many injured in the collision of the two transatlantic ships in dense fog at 11:20 last night, 45 miles south of Nantucket off the coast of Massachusetts.

50 Missing

About 50 persons were still missing and unaccounted for, but Coast Guardsmen said there may have been an error in the count.

The Andrea Doria, inbound from Mediterranean ports, and the Stockholm, outbound from New York for Europe, were traveling the great circle route when they crashed. The Stockholm, although severely damaged, picked up 533 survivors and limped toward New York.

Cause of the collision was a mystery. Both ships were equipped with radar.

Meanwhile, in Washington, Rep. Bonner (D-SC), chairman of the House Merchant Marine Committee, called on the U.S. Coast Guard for an investigation of the crash.

Bonner said reports available so far indicate that "the supposed safeguards of the lives of passengers embodied in radar and ship design and compartmentation may be insufficient."

"If this be so," Bonner said, "we must take immediate steps to determine and cure their shortcomings to avoid such future casualties which might result in great loss of life."

Newsman Dead

A survivor reported that the dead included Camille M. Cianfarra, veteran New York Times foreign correspondent, and his two children.

Dr. T.S. Peterson of Upper Montclair, N.J., who said he saw the Cianfarras dead in their cabin, also reported that his own wife was killed.

Mrs. Peterson was crushed by the impact of the vessels, he said, "and went down with the ship."

Dr. Peterson and about 750 other survivors, brought to New York by a valiant rescue ship, the French liner Ile de France, told of the hours of terror and tumult that came after the collision.

"It was just like an explosion," said Actress Ruth Roman, a survivor, "like a very big firecracker."

More than a score of stretcher cases were carried off the Ile de France after it docked in New York with its throng of shaken survivors. Many of them were cut or bruised, their faces haggard from tension.

The collision occurred in darkness and fog, touching off the greatest rescue undertaking in sea history.

While confusion and peril reigned aboard the crippled Andrea Doria, a fleet of mercy vessels—military and merchant craft—converged on the scene.

Swallowed By Sea

At 10:09 A.M. today, about 11 hours after the crash, the 29-million-dollar Andrea Doria was swallowed by the sea.

In the fear-filled interim, the throng of frantic passengers, many of them awakened from sleep and only partially dressed, crawled up the slanting decks and got down swaying nets to lifeboats sent to the ship's side.

The Andrea Doria was listing so badly she was able to launch only a few lifeboats.

"Everybody was screaming and yelling," said Valerio Monestera, a Moroccan newspaper man. "I slid down in darkness not knowing where—and then my feet touched something—it was a lifeboat."

A group of Catholic nuns, among the survivors, said they were asleep when the impact hurled them from their bunks. The same thing happened to Philadelphia mayor Richardson Dilworth and his wife.

"We put on life jackets and crawled to the boat deck," he said.

The ship was listing so heavily, passengers had to crawl on their hands and knees through the corridors and up the decks before they could get over the sides, he said.

Legs of several of the injured survivors were in casts as they were carried ashore in New York to a waiting fleet of ambulances. Some had bandages about their heads. Many wept. Some stood silently in their hurriedly-donned, mismatched clothing.

"I still don't believe it happened," said Miss

Betsy Drake, actress wife of Actor Cary Grant.…

Survivors said a few lifeboats were lowered by the Andrea Doria, although the Coast Guard had said the steep list made this impossible.

An officer said survivors may have seen lifeboats that broke loose when the ship was knocked askew.

"We heard people running outside in the halls," Dilworth said. "There was smoke in the halls…we crawled on our hands and knees through the corridors."

In the fog-blanketed darkness, lifeboats from rescue craft moved to the side of the doomed ship, while passengers—women and children first—swarmed down her high port side.

Actress Madeline Carroll, aboard the Ile de France as the massive rescue operation went on, said she "could see passengers sliding down the decks and going down rope ladders."

Fog Lifts

The heavy fog, she said, lifted "like a miracle" as the work went on in the early dawn.

A gurgling expanse of bubbles and litter marked the spot where the liner went down.

Only the swift, concerted rescue effort prevented a mass loss of life which could have surpassed the disastrous sinking of the Titanic in 1912 when 1,517 perished.

The collision ripped an enormous hole in the starboard side of the Andrea Doria and smashed the bow of the Stockholm like a flattened tin bucket.

"There was a big bang and everything flew around the room," Miss Drake said. "Suddenly the ship tilted and I threw on a robe. I was helped by a kind man who led me to the boat deck."

Everyone praised the coolness of the passengers and the work of the ship crew and officers in keeping down pandemonium.

Beatrice Bisie of Memphis, Tenn., said "There just are no words to describe the courage of the crew."

Barbara Boggs, a teen-aged girl from Manhasset, N.Y., said she was dancing in the ship's ballroom when the crash came. The lights went out, leaving the milling, yelling crowd in darkness.

In the frenzied hours—ominous with darkness and fog—frightened passengers clambered down nets or rope ladders to be hauled into lifeboats rushed to the doomed vessel's side.

"We picked up about 760 persons, many half naked, some injured, some mourning the dead," messaged Capt. Raoul de Beaudean, master of the French luxury liner, Ile de France, one of a huge armada of mercy ships.

Shortly after colliding with the Swedish liner Stockholm, *the* Andrea Doria *lists in the Atlantic Ocean. A staff photographer on board the* Ile de France *took this photo.*

Like Being In War

"Horrible.…" his message said. "Altogether it was like being back in the war."

It was on a calm but fog-shrouded sea that the multimillion dollar Andrea Doria, new queen of the Italian passenger fleet, and the Stockholm collided.

Many of the vacationing passengers were asleep when the loud, quaking impact came.

A Niagara of water poured into the gaping hole in the starboard hull of the Andrea Doria.

She gradually turned on her side until waves washed the deck. The entire bow of the Stockholm was smashed.

SOS Alarms Crackle

Desperate "SOS" alarms began crackling over the airwaves.

In one of the masterful and inspiring ventures

of seafaring, a great flotilla of rescue ships raced to the scene, launching their lifeboats to pick up the desperate, fearful throng of humanity.

"I gave an intense mental prayer for a clearing of the fog," said the message from Capt. Beaudean. "In truth the fog did start lifting and there was the Doria, quickly identifiable by her stern list."

Six other mercy ships, and a swarm of Coast Guard cutters, converged at the spot—about 45 miles from Nantucket Island—and turned it into a gigantic, Dunkirk-like rescue tableaux.

Lifeboats Overturn

Some lifeboats overturned, and doused survivors were dragged into other boats as the enormous task went on in darkness and morning haze.

Helicopters picked up five of the seriously injured, and flew them to hospitals in Boston. One was a 3-year-old Italian girl.

Cause of the violent collision was a mystery.

The Andrea Doria carried modern radar equipment which would enable it to discern another ship miles away, no matter how bad the visibility.

The smashup tore a 40-foot-wide hole in the big liner's starboard side, penetrating a third of the way through the beam, or breadth of the ship. The Andrea Doria heeled over as startled passengers rushed to upper decks.

The ship was listing so badly it could not lower its own lifeboats. Nets, ropes and other devices were strung down the port side.

For hours after the 1,134 passengers and most of the 575-man crew had left the Andrea Doria, its veteran skipper, Capt. Piero Calamai and a handful of officers remained aboard, fighting in the tradition of the sea to save their ship.

For a time, emergency pumps seemed to be keeping up with the inrushing tide of water—and at one point, the increasing list of the ship was halted. But it then became a losing battle.

Under radio orders from the line to abandon his ship if the situation became hopeless, the captain and men finally gave up. They climbed down the side of the doomed vessel to lifeboats....

■ ■ ■

Not wanting to start a panic, Captain Calamai of the *Andrea Doria* had not immediately issued an order to abandon ship after the collision. Instead, he sent out his SOS call. The first ships to arrive were a U.S. Navy transport and a freighter—too small to take all of the listing ship's passengers. The arrival of the *Ile de France* prompted a cheer from the passengers on the *Andrea Doria* and prevented a much higher death toll.

Captain Calamai wanted to preserve the tradition of going down with his ship, but his crew insisted he leave. Devastated by the accident, Calamai never sailed again.

After the accident reports on the death toll varied, and the cause of the accident was still unclear.

July 30, 1956

Doria Deaths Stay At 20; Report Errs

New York, July 29 (AP)—The Italian Line today kept its count of known dead and presumed dead on the sunken liner Andrea Doria at 20.

Earlier there had been a report from the Coast Guard that the line had raised the figure to 37.

But the line denied issuing such a figure and the Coast Guard said it had been misquoted.

There were two known dead and 18 presumed dead in the total.

List Reduced

As officer personnel at the Italian Line continued to cross-check passenger manifests and crew rosters against the names of survivors, another list of unaccounted for passengers was reduced from 73 to 45.

These were individuals believed safe but about whom no accurate information has as yet been obtained.

The Andrea Doria went to the bottom during the fogbound night of July 25 after a collision with the Stockholm about 45 miles south of Nantucket, Mass.

Dramatic rescue work by ships in the area, abetted by Coast Guard vessels, saved most of the

1,706 passengers and crewmen reported aboard the 30,000-ton Doria.

The 12,600-ton Stockholm, her bow slashed to ribbons by the impact with the forward starboard side of the Doria, stayed afloat after the crash and effected the rescue of more than 500 persons from the ill-fated Italian ship.

The morning after its collision with the Stockholm, *the* Andrea Doria *takes its final plunge into the ocean.*

Figures Vary

The Swedish ship now is in a Brooklyn drydock for repairs. Two of the vessel's crewmen died in the crash and three other crew members are missing and presumed dead.

Figures concerning fatalities and those rescued have varied since the Doria went down.

Tabulations by the Italian Line, the New York City Police Department, and the Coast Guard all have varied.

The Doria, after leaving her home port of Genoa for the westbound voyage, made stops at Naples, Cannes, and Gibraltar, taking on passengers at each place.

All records reportedly went down with the ship, including the navigation, radio and radar logs.

The American Red Cross, which has been busy distributing clothing and money to many survivors, is continuing efforts to trace persons about whom it had received inquiries from friends and relatives.

The Red Cross emphasized it was furnishing aid and information wherever possible but was not engaged in compiling a full list of the missing.

Skin divers reported yesterday the Andrea Doria is lying in about 250 feet of water. The divers said they saw a great deal of debris but no signs of bodies.

Both the Stockholm and Doria were equipped with radar.

Neither Capt. Gunnar Nordenson, skipper of the Stockholm, nor Capt. Piero Calamai, master of the Doria, has commented on the cause of the collision.

Swedish Line officials have said the Stockholm's radar was working before and after the crash....

■ ■ ■

The Italian Line and the Swedish-American Line went to court, blaming each other for the crash. Investigations revealed the two ships shared the fault.

Neither the *Andrea Doria* nor the *Stockholm* had reduced its speed by half, as required in fog. The *Stockholm's* only officer on the bridge was inexperienced, and the ship was using the wrong sea lane for westward travel. The *Doria* had not refilled empty water and oil tanks with sea water, which might have helped prevent the severe listing caused by the collision. Finally, Captain Calamai made the peculiar decision to steer his ship to the left when he realized the *Doria* and the *Stockholm* were heading for each other. Sea regulations call for ships to turn to the right, which the *Stockholm* did. Calamai's maneuver, plus the dense fog, sealed his ship's fate.

The Italian Line had also worried about publicly revealing a mechanical flaw: the *Doria* had a faulty watertight door. That door, however, did not play a part in the ship's sinking. A series of dives into the wreck of the *Doria* showed that the *Stockholm* had destroyed that door in the collision.

The two shipping companies eventually settled out of court.

United Airlines-TWA Midair Collision

**Brooklyn, New York
December 16, 1960
Death Toll: 136**

The first midair collision in the history of U.S. commercial aviation took place over the Grand Canyon in 1956. All 128 people aboard the planes were killed. Pilots at the time often flew over the canyon to give their passengers a look at the spectacular view. In the 1956 crash the pilots were in airspace not monitored by radar. The accident led to changes in safety rules, but those changes did not prevent another disastrous midair collision just four years later.

December 17, 1960

134 Die As 2 Airliners Collide, Rain Wreckage on New York; Toll Sets Mark

Boy Lone Survivor; Debris Misses School

NEW YORK (AP)—Two airliners, one a jet, collided in the air Friday and plunged into New York City. There were 134 persons killed in the worst disaster in the history of aviation.

Not since the Wright brothers gave wings to mankind in 1903 has there been a single air catastrophe to equal the blazing collision that scorched the air below it.

Of 128 persons aboard the two planes, the sole survivor was one small boy.

The jet plunged into a crowded Brooklyn neighborhood, killing a street cleaner at work and six other persons. A block-wide area was scourged with fiery death and destruction.

The other plane, a four-engine, propeller-driven craft, apparently exploded and came down in flaming pieces on Staten Island, across the narrow neck of New York Harbor. It landed in an open field, sparing further tragedy.

Police fixed the collision spot above the Narrows, the heavily traveled steamship lane between Brooklyn and Staten Island. Federal authorities said the jet's last reported position was 5,000 feet over Preston, N.J., while the other plane was cleared over Linden, N.J., to drop down from 6,000 to 5,000 feet.

Points Out Peril

Until now, the worst air tragedy in history was the death of 129 servicemen in the June 18, 1953, crash near Tokyo of an American Air Force transport.

Fire Commissioner Edward P. Cavanagh Jr., said it might be many hours before all the buildings ravaged by the fallen jet could be thoroughly searched for bodies.

The awesome tragedy, occurring over a metropolitan area, pointed up the growing peril of overcrowded airways above the nation's larger cities.

It was only the second in-flight collision between commercial airliners. The last was over the Grand Canyon in Arizona in 1956 when all 128 persons died in a collision between a Trans World Airlines plane and a United airliner.

By grim coincidence, the same two airlines were involved in Friday's crash. It occurred at 10:34 a.m. in dirty gray skies that were further obscured by falling snow. The two big planes were coming from the west for separate landings at the two New York City airports—La Guardia Field and Idlewild Airport, about 10 miles apart on Long Island. The ceiling was about 600 feet.

Search for Clues

The two planes were supposed to have been at different altitudes. But for some unexplained reason, they weren't. Recorded conversations their pilots had with the control towers were being monitored for some clue to the tragedy. So was an automatic flight recording device carried by jets to list their action in flight.

Ironically, a part of the jetliner came to rest in the wreckage of a Brooklyn funeral parlor, with a score or more passengers entombed in the debris of the house of death.

Would-be rescuers told of seeing passengers' bodies held to their seats by safety belts they had affixed in anticipation of landing. In the past, many passenger lives have been saved in air mishaps by just such belts. But this time the fury of the disaster made them worthless.

Many of the passengers were coming home for Christmas. They bore gaily wrapped holiday gifts for relatives and friends.

Hours after the crash, dusk's merciful effort to black out the horror of the Brooklyn scene was thwarted by the garish glare of huge police and fire department searchlights. They played over the wreckage as it was being probed for victims.

Misses Packed School

Residents made homeless by the crash were fed and sheltered at a nearby public school and in the auditorium of St. Augustine's Roman Catholic church.

In its anguished death plunge, the big jet narrowly missed St. Augustine School, adjoining the church. There were 1,700 pupils at classes inside. Brother Brendan of the school staff said: "It appeared the pilot made a deliberate effort to avoid striking the spire of the church."

The UAL plane was the first passenger-carrying jet to crash in this country since the inauguration of the jet age of U.S. commercial aviation two years ago.

The jet was UAL Flight 826 which left Chicago at 8:11 a.m. It was bound for Idlewild on the South Shore of Long Island, due there at 10:45 a.m. with 77 passengers and a crew of seven.

It came down in a crowded Brooklyn area of shops and apartments, setting 10 buildings afire and demolishing a church—ironically named "Pillar of Fire." The superior of St. Augustine's, the spared Catholic school, saw the plane crash. He immediately took over the public address system and led the 1,700 pupils in recitation of the rosary for the victims of the crash.

A huge mass of flames and a billowing cloud of

oily black smoke marked the jet's bier and spread fiery ruin through the area.

One Known Survivor

Incredibly, there was one known survivor among the airborne passengers—Stephen Baltz, 11, of Chicago, on his way here to join his mother in a visit to relatives. He was badly burned. His watch had stopped at 9:37, Chicago time.

Mayor Robert F. Wagner hurried to the Brooklyn scene, later to report: "It was very bad. Most of the bodies are horribly mutilated."

The other plane in the collision, TWA's Lockheed Constellation Flight 266, headed for La Guardia on the North Shore of Long Island from Dayton, Ohio. It took off at 7:40 a.m. and was due in at 10:40 a.m. with 39 passengers and a crew of five. Six survived the crash, but all died soon after.

As it came apart with horrifying force, the TWA plane spewed an area of Staten Island with flaming debris. It came down in an open area of fields and trees after skimming over a row of bungalows.

Firefighters probe some of the wreckage that landed on Staten Island, New York, after the 1960 midair collision between a United and a TWA plane.

Describes Horror

The horror of its plunge was graphically described by Clifford Beuth, an oil deliveryman.

"I saw the engine on the right side blow up. Then the second engine on the right side blew up and as it did it blew the tail section to pieces. I saw a couple of people falling out of the plane as it was falling. The plane was on fire from the time it blew up to the time it crashed."

The TWA plane was being monitored on radar during its approach to La Guardia. Suddenly its image disappeared from the screen.

The UAL jetliner was on instruments as it groped down through the murk toward Idlewild.

The criss-cross landing and takeoff operation is performed scores of times each day over New York as planes utilize its two busy Long Island airports. Normally, however, planes bound for La Guardia are assigned to a different altitude than those using Idlewild.

"Obviously something went wrong, but we don't know what," said an airport source at Idlewild.

An airline passenger agent at Idlewild, a red-haired young woman, said "We told them what has happened, and they know that the plane has crashed. We have no details and so we can't tell them much more."

Details Lacking

Details of the tragedy were indeed scant. George R. Baker of the Civil Aeronautics Bureau, one of the investigators on the Brooklyn scene, said not only was the cause of the crash unknown, but so was the actual area where the two planes collided.

"We have to start from scratch," he declared.

As he spoke with reporters, firemen nearby tore at the wreckage of the United airliner in quest of bodies. They wore heavy canvas gloves to shield their hands from the hot and jagged metal.

Smoke, swirling this way and that from the plane and the burning buildings, obscured the figures of the fire fighters from time to time. Tongues of flame licked from windows in the burning buildings.

Hundreds of firemen, policemen, doctors, nurses and ambulance attendants swarmed into the Brooklyn area. A vacant store and a tailor shop saw service as improvised morgues during removal of the victims' bodies.

From Washington, the American Red Cross

dispatched its national director of disaster services, Enzo Bighinatti, to New York. And from Dayton came E.R. Quesada, administrator of the Federal Aviation Agency, to join in the investigation of the tragedy....

■ ■ ■

Idlewild Airport, the destination of the United jet, is today known as John F. Kennedy International Airport.

The day after the accident officials still were not sure why the planes had crashed.

December 18, 1960

Clues to Deadly Error Sought in Dual Crash

NEW YORK (AP)—History's worst air disaster took on an added note of heartbreak Saturday as investigators began a sweeping hunt for the elusive error—or malfunction—that caused two planes to collide in the air.

Only a few fragmentary hints emerged.

As they did, new grief struck. Of the 128 aboard the two doomed planes, one passenger, Stephen Baltz, 11, Wilmette, Ill., had clung to life for more than 24 hours.

But he died Saturday, of burns and inhaled flames. And Friday's thanksgiving of his parents, who had stood watch at his hospital bedside, turned to tears.

All Perished

The over-all toll of death thus rose to 137 from the collision that rained fiery destruction on the city. All aboard both planes perished, along with nine others on the ground.

Police said still more bodies may lie in the wreckage and torn buildings.

As the broad, rapid-fire inquiry proceeded, these inklings of what happened were indicated:

One plane was being watched on radar. The other apparently was not. One must have been off course.

Both planes, a United Air Lines DC8 jet and a Trans World Airlines four-engine Constellation, were descending for a landing when their paths inextricably crossed.

A top federal aviation official said that under such circumstances, "if both planes were under positive control at the time one was off course."

Phillip Goldstein, chief of the investigating division of the Civil Aeronautics Board, also said the TWA plane was being traced at La Guardia Field, its destination.

As for the jet, headed for Idlewild Airport 10 miles away, he said: "I don't believe that the United Air Lines plane had been identified as such on the scope."

The hard-pressed CAB investigation was described as the most extensive ever undertaken by the agency.

It brought a vast corps of experts here, many of them working through the night examining radio communications records, plane remnants, charred equipment, flight patterns and other material in a search for the cause.

"So far there is no definite lead," Goldstein said.

At the same time, nearly 300 police and firemen still dug through the ruins in a crowded Brooklyn neighborhood where the huge jet plane fell, gouging walls, shearing roofs, and setting a dozen structures afire.

92 Bodies Recovered

Altogether, 92 bodies have been recovered there, 83 of them presumably plane victims, the other nine killed on the ground. Baltz' death brought the jet crash toll to 93, counting those killed on the ground.

On Staten Island, where the exploding TWA plane scattered along the eastern shore, bodies of 43 of the 44 known killed—all on the plane—have been found.

Most of the bodies remained individually unidentified, and the grisly task of doing so progressed slowly. In many cases, because of disfigurement, it was necessary to rely on fingerprints or other laboratory methods.

An FBI team was aiding in the process.

The double crash surpassed in deaths the previous high of 129 killed on an Air Force C124 Globemaster near Tokyo, June 18, 1953.

It also was the first crash in America of a pure jet airliner carrying passengers.

The mystery of how it occurred brought the combined forces of the CAB and the Federal Aviation Agency into action, and so far, the clues were only tentative.

"It could have been human error to which we are all subject," said E.R. Quesada, head of the agency. He said the two approaching planes "should not have come closer than three miles."

But for some reason, the complex and elaborate system that is used for guiding the congested air traffic above the city didn't work in this case.

Quesada said no evidence had been found of any mechanical malfunction. But also, no human blame has been assessed. It could have been either, in countless ways.

Rescue workers crowd a Brooklyn street after the tail section of the United jet (foreground) crashed to the ground.

Sky Obscured

With traffic moving in and out of the two New York fields, plus nearby Newark, N.J., Airport and several surrounding air bases, many planes must be directed at once. They are supposed to be assigned different altitudes and separately timed approaches to keep them apart.

Snow and fog obscured the skies when the two ill-fated airliners rammed, veering off to their graves on opposite sides of New York Harbor.

They were operating "on instruments" under such weather conditions, Quesada said.

Incoming planes usually are guided by the air traffic control center at Idlewild until they near their destinations. Then control is transferred to the specific airport where they are to land.

Somewhere, by human error or failure of instruments, the two planes roared together in the murk.

The fury of the impact aloft was underlined when one of the jet engines of the United Air Lines plane that fell in Brooklyn was found amid the far-flung wreckage of the TWA plane on Staten Island.

"This confirms that an air collision occurred," said G. Joseph Minetti, of the CAB.

Jet Hurled Free

The jet engine apparently lodged in the ripped TWA plane structure, or was hurled free of the jet, as the two planes came together, and then whipped apart, diving to earth in flames.

Being studied in the investigation are tapes of the radio conversations between the control towers and the pilots during the fateful interval when the planes should have been kept on separate levels and approach points.

Also under study is a fire-blackened instrument box from the wrecked jetliner, containing a device that records the plane's altitude, speed and position at all times. Officials expressed hope this record would be undamaged.

Goldstein said the investigators felt confident "that we should be able to find the probable cause" of the accident, but details of the facts discovered would not be made public until a hearing is held. The final answer, if one is found, might not come for many days.

So far, Goldstein said there has been no evidence of any mechanical failure on either plane, nor have any messages from either been reported indicating they were in trouble before the collision.

■ ■ ■ ■

A few days later government officials disclosed that the United jet had been 11 miles off course as it approached Idlewild.

The instrument box mentioned in the article is now sometimes called the "black box." In an airplane accident the black box provides key information about possible causes of a crash. In this case the Federal Aviation Agency (FAA—later the Federal Aviation Administration) eventually found that the crew of the United jet had been largely responsible. They had failed to report that one of their navigation devices was not working correctly. Also, a lack of direct communication between the two airports increased the risk of disaster. The two airlines and the government paid $29 million in damages to relatives of the victims.

After this second TWA-United crash the FAA once again introduced new safety regulations. The speed limit for planes approaching airports was reduced, and commercial airliners were required to carry TACAN, a radio navigation system that had been developed for military use.

Sinking of the *Thresher*

Off the Coast of New England
April 10, 1963
Death Toll: 129

A Dutch inventor, Cornelius van Drebbel, is credited with building the first working *submarine*—a ship that could sail underwater—in the early 17th century. More than 100 years later David Bushnell, an American, created the *Turtle,* a one-man craft, and in 1776 it was used for the first submarine attack on a surface ship. After that subs were mainly used for warfare, though it took until the 20th century to perfect them. Still, like any ships, subs are prone to mechanical failures, and when something goes wrong underwater, there's little hope for the sailors on board. In 1939 the crew of the British sub *Thetis* discovered that danger when a malfunction sank the craft, killing 99 out of the 103 people on board.

In 1954 the United States began a new era of subs, launching the *Nautilus,* the world's first nuclear-powered sub. With nuclear power submarines could stay submerged for weeks at a time. Within a decade the U.S. had greatly expanded its fleet of nuclear submarines, and the *Thresher* was one of the country's newest examples of that technology.

April 11, 1963

Atomic Sub Carrying 129 Feared Lost In Test 220 Miles East of N. England

Navy Says Oil Sighted After Dive by Thresher

WASHINGTON (AP)—The atomic submarine Thresher, carrying 129 men, vanished Wednesday after a steep test dive in the Atlantic. The Navy said it "appears to be lost." The Navy said an oil slick had been sighted—the traditional sign that a submarine has met disaster. A flicker of hope remained that the Thresher may have surfaced in rough waters and was having communications trouble.

An attack sub designed for use against other submarines and surface vessels, the Thresher last was heard from at 9:17 a.m. Eastern Standard Time on Wednesday. There was no word from her 12 hours later—when the Navy reported the sighting of the oil slick.

The sub was in a deep test dive and apparently failed to come up.

The craft was missing some 220 miles east of Boston—in an area where the ocean is 8,400 feet deep. Underwater pressure at that depth makes rescue impossible, the Navy said, even if a submarine could survive the hydraulic force.

Adm. George W. Anderson, chief of naval operations, said there was "absolutely no chance of nuclear explosion in the submarine, nor is there any danger of radioactive contamination" to shipping.

The Thresher, as an attack submarine, does not carry Polaris missiles.

Anderson, who talked to newsmen at the Pentagon, said, "To those of us who have been brought up in the traditions of the sea it is a sad occasion when a ship is reported lost."

There have been many underwater disasters, but the mighty nuclear-powered U.S. submarine fleet has been remarkably free from accidents since the first of the new underwater craft, the Nautilus, was launched more than a decade ago.

Rated as Fastest

The Thresher was rated as the world's fastest and deepest-diving submarine.

Although she did not pack the nuclear-tipped Polaris, she was equipped with torpedoes and a variety of other underwater weapons.

The Thresher's exact diving capability is a secret, but it obviously is not designed to operate at anywhere near 8,400 feet. The Navy merely said the lengthy test dive was at depths in excess of 400 feet.

Accompanied by the submarine rescue ship Skylark, the Thresher began its dive at 12:22 p.m. Tuesday about 30 miles south of Portsmouth, N.H. After six hours, the Thresher was to have come up nearer the surface and then continue its test operations. But the Skylark heard nothing from the Thresher after 9:17 a.m.

There was no indication of suspicious unidentified submarines or surface vessels in the immediate area, the Navy said.

The Navy ordered an extensive air and sea rescue operation, but its movements were hindered by clouds, winds of about 30 to 45 miles per hour and waves five to nine feet high.

The Thresher had undergone overhaul and was carrying 17 civilians on a test run. The Navy said the ship also carried 16 officers and 96 enlisted men.

Routine Procedure

It was routine procedure to send another submarine rescue ship along with the Thresher on the diving tests.

The Navy at first said the Thresher was "overdue and presumed missing," but after the oil slick was sighted, changed this to "appears to be lost."

"The location of the Thresher from her last report was given as 41.44 north and 64.57 west," the Navy said. "The depth of water at this location is approximately 8,400 feet. Merchant ships in this area have been requested to keep a sharp lookout for the submarine in addition to the maximum effort being made by the Navy."

The loss of life would make it the worst peacetime submarine disaster ever recorded.

By comparison, the last U.S. submarine to be lost in peacetime—the Squalus—carried 59 aboard. It went down in 240 feet of water off the New Hampshire coast. Thirty-three aboard were rescued, and the submarine subsequently was raised and returned to service. That was in 1939, before the atomic age.

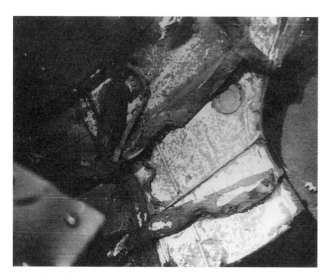

A section of the nuclear-powered submarine Thresher *lies on the ocean floor off of Massachusetts. This picture was taken by sailors on board the underwater search vessel* Trieste *during its second series of dives to find the missing sub.*

Cruised Under Arctic

Nuclear submarines have traveled thousands of miles underwater without even sending up a snorkel—the breathing-tube device used in World War II. They have cruised under the Arctic ice cap.

Two conventionally powered submarines were lost in accidents since World War II. The Cochina sank in the North Atlantic in August 1949 after fire broke out. Another sub removed the crew.

In 1958, the submarine Stickleback was sunk after colliding with a destroyer near the entrance to Pearl Harbor. All hands were saved.

Asked if changes now will be made in the atomic sub program, Anderson replied: "This is

part of the penalty we pay in developing the fine submarine forces we have today."

A board of investigation, headed by Vice Adm. Bernard Austin, commandant of the Naval War College at Newport, R.I., has been appointed, Anderson said.

Delay Explained

He was asked why the Navy delayed any announcement of the disappearance of the submarine until hours after the Thresher made her last report.

He said the Navy did not want to alarm families of the men aboard, and also there was the possibility the submarine's radio system had failed and she was unable to report.

Anderson said there was no possibility of recovering parts of the Thresher, if she went down to 8,400 feet. However, he said the Navy is considering using the deep-diving experimental submarine Trieste, now on the West Coast, to go down in the area and see what can be found by observation.

Among the ships searching the area are five additional destroyers—Yarnell, Wallace Lind, Warrington, the Sullivans, S.B. Roberts—the frigate Norfolk and submarines Sea Wolf and Sea Owl. Another submarine rescue ship Sunbird was expected to reach the area later.

Flying overhead are four P2 Neptune patrol aircraft from Brunswick, Maine. More planes were expected.

During the diving test there is no requirement that the two crafts maintain constant communication, the Navy said, but after the Thresher failed to report at the scheduled time the Skylark began calling her on the underwater communication system.

The Thresher is 278 feet long, 31 feet, 8 inches wide, displaces 3,700 tons when surfaced and 4,311 tons under water. She was launched July 9, 1960, and commissioned Aug. 3, 1961.

There are two other subs of the Thresher class in the fleet—the Permit and the Plunger.

■ ■ ■

Navy Sifts Clues To Find Out Why Atomic Sub Sank

May Use TV to Scan Sub's Hull

WASHINGTON (AP)—The Navy intends to go ahead with construction of 22 more submarines like the lost Thresher, but is making a new study of the entire structural design, Secretary Fred Korth said Friday.

Korth told newsmen the design study for this class ship, begun by the Bureau of Ships, is aside from and in addition to the general investigation by a naval court of inquiry into the whole subject of the loss of the Thresher.

This investigation includes inquiry into the structural integrity of the Thresher after her overhaul in the Portsmouth, N.H., Navy Yard.

Will Scan Bottom

As part of this investigation, the Navy said Friday it may use underwater television to scan the sunken nuclear submarine if its hulk is located at the bottom of the Atlantic.

The Navy has embarked on a methodical and painstaking course in its effort to find out what sent the newly overhauled craft to the bottom with all aboard: 129 men.

Korth returned Thursday night from talks with officials in Portsmouth and Groton, Conn. He also flew over the scene of the sinking and talked by radio with officials aboard the search ships.

Officially Dead

The Navy secretary announced officially Thursday night that the Thresher and her crew were lost, an act which has the effect of declaring the 129 persons aboard the submarine legally dead instead of missing.

Korth said he did this for two reasons: 1. because "we shouldn't hold out hope for the dependents" of the men when there was absolutely no chance that they were alive, and 2. to clear the way for a prompt beginning on payment of death benefits and collection of insurance.

Some speculation was reported in Congress over whether construction of another attack submarine should be authorized to replace, numerically, the lost Thresher.

Asked for Eight

Korth said he was unaware of this, but he did recall that the Navy initially asked for eight atomic-powered attack submarines under the fiscal 1964 program. The Defense Department reduced this to six; the House voted authorization for eight, the Senate six. The difference now is to compromise.

Rear Adm. John S. McCain Jr., Navy information chief, said deep-probing sonar equipment is being used to try to locate the Thresher 220 miles east of Cape Cod.

Twelve vessels are in the search area and McCain said they will be joined by four others, including the Polaris missile submarine Thomas Jefferson. Oceanographers were on the scene, using special echo sound gear to draw a sort of road map of the bottom, a mile and half down.

There was no sense of urgency. All hope for the 129 men aboard was gone.…

■ ■ ■

The Navy brought in a special underwater craft, a *bathyscaph*, to continue the search for the *Thresher*. The bathyscaph, called the *Trieste*, was capable of plunging almost 7 miles below the ocean's surface. Several months after the accident the *Trieste* found the remains of the *Thresher* about 8,000 feet below sea level. According to the Navy, sea water had leaked into the sub and flooded the engine room. As the sub sank, the increased water pressure at the lower depths turned the sub's hull into a twisted wreck.

Three-Way Train Collision

Yokohama, Japan
November 9, 1963
Death Toll: 162

Japan built its first railway in 1872. Before World War II the country was not a world leader in modern train travel, but after the war Japan modernized its rail system as part of the general, phenomenal industrialization of the country. A greater reliance on railways also created deadlier railway accidents, including this November 9, 1963, three-way collision.

November 10, 1963

Japan Day of Disaster; 482 Die

155 Killed In Train Wreck

YOKOHAMA, Japan (AP)—Three trains, two of them jammed with weekend commuters, crashed in a tower of smoke and flame Saturday night. Steel and human bodies were shredded like paper.

Police said the death toll this morning stood at 155, including one American. More than 60 persons were injured, many seriously, and officials feared the death toll would climb.

One passenger train speeding through the rainy night from this port city to Tokyo crashed into a derailed freight train. The passenger train then swerved across the tracks and knifed into another commuter train speeding south.

Trapped In Wreckage

Steel sliced through steel, telescoping cars and mangling passengers in their seats. Power lines along the tracks tumbled in a flash of light and then darkness fell as screaming passengers tumbled out of the trains.

Many victims were trapped in the twisted wreckage and firemen had to cut their way in with torches. Emergency searchlights cast an unearthly glow as rescuers looked for survivors.

The only known American victim was 28-year-old William Scott, whose father, Harold L. Scott, lives at Colorado Springs, Colo. The younger Scott was a student of Japanese language and history at Tokyo International Christian University in Tokyo.

Scott's body was taken to an incense-filled Buddhist temple, which was turned into a temporary morgue. Scores of Japanese bodies were there also and the sobs and moans of Japanese women and children filled the air. Priests chanted prayers.

Japanese reporters and photographers watch as rescue workers search for survivors after the three-train accident near Yokohama in 1963.

Hospitals Jammed

Thirteen hospitals called in their entire staffs to care for the injured.

U.S. Navy Medical Corpsmen from the American base at nearby Yokosuka worked side by side with Japanese police, firemen and soldiers in rescue operations.

Shoes, clothing and scuffed brief cases littered the tracks at the Tsurumi crossing between Tokyo and Yokohama.

The accident occurred at 9:40 p.m.

The conductor of the freight train, Masami Sugimoto, 46, said he was knocked to the floor when the cars jumped the track.

"I ran along the Yokosuka line toward Tokyo

about 50 yards, and lit a smoke candle hoping to prevent the commuter train from crashing into the derailed train," the conductor said.

"It was all in vain. The commuter crashed into the freight. I could not see anything because of the mushrooming dust."

Kenzo Otani, whose house overlooks the scene, ran outdoors when the first passenger train hit the derailed freight.

"Then, immediately, the train from Yokosuka rammed into the derailed train and I watched telephone poles collapse in a big column of fire."

Saw No Signal

Shinji Wakabayashi, 37, who was at the controls of the electric-powered commuter train racing south from Tokyo to Yokohama and bound for Yokosuka, said he did not see the smoke from the candle.

"The moment we began to pass by the incoming train, there was a tremendous shock. I grabbed the emergency brake.

"The moment my train stopped, I jumped down and found the fourth and fifth coach of my train had been smashed by the first (powered) coach on the incoming train."

What he didn't know at the time was that the Tokyo-bound train had hit the derailed freight and then careened across the roadbed into the middle cars of his train.

It was Japan's third worst train disaster since World War II and the second three-train wreck in 18 months. Two commuter trains and a freight piled up near Mikawashima May 3, 1962, killing 160 persons and injuring 300 more. In February, 1947, 184 persons died when a train overturned west of Tokyo....

■ ■ ■

November 9, 1963, was a bleak day for Japan, as another disaster took hundreds of lives. In Omuta a coal-mine explosion killed more than 400 Japanese miners (see Volume 8, *Nuclear and Industrial Disasters*). The following day two more trains collided, but this time the damage was slight.

Japan Is Spared A Third Disaster

2 Injured In Another Rail Crash

Mine, Wreck Toll Mounts

TOKYO (AP)—A crowded express train rammed into the rear of a second express near Hiroshima Sunday but the nation was spared another disaster. Just two persons were injured, officials said.

The new accident came as Japan mourned more than 600 dead in a coal mine explosion and a triple train wreck Saturday.

National Railway officials said both trains in the new collision were only a half mile out of a station and that one was halted while the other was moving at low speed.

The site of the crash was between the towns of Motoyura and Koto, west of Hiroshima, the city where the first atomic bomb was dropped in World War II.

Busy Hour

The wreck occurred at a time when Japanese trains are normally crowded. Involved were the Asakaze express and the Mizuho express of the Japan National Railway's Santo Line.

On Saturday, 162 persons were killed in a triple train wreck 15 miles south of Tokyo that occurred just six hours after a coal mine explosion on the southern island of Kyushu took the lives of 448 miners....

As the news of the explosion at Japan's largest and most modern mine spread across the nation, disaster struck again. A packed passenger train speeding toward Tokyo smashed into a derailed freight train, then leaped across the tracks into the fourth and fifth cars of a commuter train coming from the opposite direction.

Steel coaches were slashed and crumpled. Some of the bodies were so badly mangled that positive identification was only possible through fingerprinting....

The cause of the original freight derailment still was not known.

The accident occurred at one of the busiest sectors of the Japanese rail system. And the two passenger trains bore down on the freight within half a minute of the derailment.

Some mourners accosted Reisuke Ishida, president of Japan National Railways, as he moved amid rows of coffins at a Buddhist temple near the wreck. But the grief-stricken official could give no reply to their demands for an explanation of the accident.

Earlier, he said he accepted full responsibility and would offer his resignation to Prime Minister Hayato Ikeda.

The combined death toll of the two accidents was the highest since 1954 when an overcrowded ferry boat capsized in a typhoon off the island of Hokkaido and 1,172 drowned, including 56 Americans....

Three young American sailors survived the train wreck. They were heading back to their ships at Yokosuka after a visit to Tokyo when the passenger train smashed into the two cars directly behind theirs.

The sailors, all Californians, were Fireman Jimmy Bolin of 111 Ameluxen Ave., La Bunte; Fireman William B. Ullerick of 9836 Rincon Ave., Arleta, and Seaman Larry G. Pacheco of 6320 Ethel Ave., Van Nuys.

They carried about 20 injured from the wreckage and then helped remove some of the bodies of victims.

Ullerick said one of the ill-fated coaches was so badly torn apart it looked like a flatbed car.

"Bodies were piled up on the right side of the car four to six deep. Bolin, Pacheco and I crawled through the car and started carrying people who seemed to be alive."

■ ■ ■

As Japan mourned the more than 600 people killed in the Yokohama train wreck and the Omuta mine explosion, members of the country's leftist parties claimed the government was responsible for the accidents. Japan was approaching a national election, and the leftists turned the accidents into political issues, charging that Japanese leaders were emphasizing big business and profits at the expense of public safety. Despite the accusations, the ruling party easily retained power.

The rash of train accidents, going back to the May 3, 1962, crash mentioned in the first news report, did not slow Japan's ambitious railway plans. In 1966 the country opened its *Shinkansen* train service. These so-called "bullet" trains reached speeds of 125 miles per hour. Today, they can reach up to 160 miles per hour, and Japan has remained a pioneer in high-speed rail travel.

Mexican National Railways Train Derailment

Saltillo, Mexico
October 5, 1972
Death Toll: 208

In 1972 four countries had major train accidents. On June 4 two trains collided in Bangladesh, killing 76. Less than two weeks later two French trains collided, killing more than 100. In July a train collision in Spain also killed 76 people. The last and worst of the year's major railway accidents took place in Mexico.

October 7, 1972

Mexican Rail Crash Kills More Than 140

SALTILLO, Mexico (AP)—A train speeding down a hill with about 1,600 religious pilgrims aboard derailed and caught fire, killing 149 persons and injuring 781, police reported Friday.

A spokesman for the Mexican National Railways said a preliminary investigation showed the train was traveling about 75 m.p.h., at the time of the accident, twice the speed permitted on a downhill curve such as the train was approaching.

The official said the brakes apparently functioned, but could not slow the train sufficiently because of the speed. The drivers of the two engines pulling the 22-car train were only slightly injured and were being questioned by authorities.

Rescuers search through the night for survivors of the 1972 train derailment in Saltillo, Mexico.

Survivors said the train had been approaching the Moreno Bridge south of Saltillo about midnight Thursday when the engine overturned and several cars jammed together and caught fire. Some entire families were reported killed.

A team of 150 rescuers worked through the day searching for survivors in the wreckage. By afternoon Police and Transit Director Genaro Gutierrez Davila said everyone known to have been trapped had been rescued.

The pilgrims were returning from Catorce in northern San Luis Potosi state, where they had gone to pray to St. Francis.

■ ■ ■

October 8, 1972

Train Toll Up; Alcohol Suspected

SALTILLO, Mexico (AP)—The death toll in the train wreck near here rose to 165 Saturday, and authorities said blood tests indicated the engineer had been drinking.

A spokesman for the National Railroads said the brakes of the train were in perfect condition but the train was traveling at about 70 miles per hour—twice the speed allowed on the downhill curve where it derailed.

A survivor said the train roared down the hill "like a wild animal" before the derailment Thursday night.

The engineer, identified as Melchor Sanchez, and five other crew members were placed under arrest.

Damaged railway cars are scattered around the site where the Mexican passenger train—traveling at twice the permitted speed—jumped the tracks.

At the crash scene, rescuers were trying to reach one of the railroad cars still buried Saturday in the rubble nearly two days after the accident.

Earlier Saturday three persons were found alive in the wreckage, pushing the number of injured to 1,011, Police Chief Genaro Gutierrez Davila of Coahulla State reported. Some survivors underwent amputations in order to be freed.

The train, which derailed six miles south of Saltillo, ended up with cars piled on top of one another. Some victims died in the pileup, others in the fire which broke out in four of the 24 cars.

■ ■ ■

When survivors found the drunk engineer at the accident scene, they tried to lynch him on the spot. A railroad official stopped the mob from killing the engineer, who had been drinking with other crew members while driving the train.

Turkish Airlines Crash

Paris, France
March 3, 1974
Death Toll: 346

By 1974 the highest death toll from an aviation disaster was 176 people; the crash of a Turkish jetliner near Paris nearly doubled that number. Shortly after takeoff, flying at almost 500 miles an hour, a McDonnell-Douglas DC-10 suddenly lost radio contact with air-traffic controllers on the ground.

March 4, 1974

Worst Plane Crash In History Kills 346

Turkish Jet Rams Slope Near Paris

PARIS (AP)—A packed Turkish jetliner slammed into a wooded slope and exploded north of Paris Sunday, spewing debris and bodies for miles in the worst air disaster in history. An airline official said all 346 aboard were killed.

"It exploded with a great roar," said a witness.

Bodies hung from trees and parts of bodies were scattered in the forest around the bits and pieces of the airplane. Six bodies were recovered nine miles from the site.

Argun Yelutas, European manager of Turkish Airlines, said 334 passengers and 12 crewmen were aboard the trijet DC10. He said 200 to 250 names could be British or American.

United Press International quoted airline sources Sunday night as saying five passengers may have been guerrillas carrying bombs that exploded in flight.

The sources said the airline had information indicating three Japanese and two Arabs who boarded the plane at Paris for the flight to London were guerrillas.

They said according to their information the guerrillas had planned to sabotage a British Airways flight from Paris to London but the flight was canceled, they were transferred to the Turkish plane and their bombs exploded after takeoff, causing the crash.

The jet had taken off from Orly Airport five minutes earlier after a stop on its flight from Istanbul to London. Yelutas said the takeoff was normal and the skies clear, but when the plane reached 13,000 feet, "there was no more news."

A French fireman inspects the mangled main section of the Turkish Airlines jet that crashed near Paris in 1974.

The secretary of state of the French transportation ministry, Aymar Achille-Fould, said: "The fact that debris and bodies were found in a village more than 10 kilometers (six miles) from the accident tends to prove that the explosion occurred in flight."

Several witnesses said they saw the plane burst into flames after it crashed. Others said they heard an explosion, but it could not be determined whether it was before or after the wide-bodied jet hit the ground.

Rescue workers continued poking into the turf as night fell, finding only bright magazine pictures, electrical parts and the endless, meaningless accessories to the lives of the 346 persons.

Maurice Lhote, who works at the Le Bourget control tower and was out for a Sunday walk in the forest with his family, said he saw the plane in difficulty. He added, "I heard no explosion on board before the accident."

Another witness said, "I saw the plane literally plunge into the forest. It was only after two or three seconds that I seemed to hear an explosion. Immediately there was a terrible blast of air."

Another witness said he ran to the crash scene right after the 181-foot-long airliner plummeted into the woods.

"Through the black smoke I saw blood, blood everywhere," he said. "Bits of bodies, scarred trees, shreds of metal. It was horrible."

Bodies in Undergrowth

Pieces of the red-and-white plane jammed between trees. Cushions and other material from the interior hung draped over the stark winter branches. Parts of bodies were buried in the undergrowth.

Rescuers carried away bodies in blankets and paper bags. Firemen said that when the American-made plane broke up into small pieces, it flattened a part of the forest, a favorite picnic ground for Parisians.

Rescuers reported strollers in a field nine miles south of the main wreckage found seven bodies. Helicopters hovered over the area to look for the scattered bodies and debris.

Some recovered bodies were so disfigured that firemen on the scene expressed doubt they could ever be identified.…

■ ■ ■

The rise of terrorism in the Middle East during the 1970s, often with planes as the targets (see Volume 2, *Civil Unrest and Terrorism*), aroused suspicion that the DC-10 crash was also the result of terrorism. Aviation officials explored that angle as they searched for clues about the crash.

March 5, 1974

Probe Under Way In Jetliner Crash

PARIS (AP)—Experts were investigating Monday the possibility that a bomb may have blown up the Turkish jetliner which crashed near Paris in the worst air disaster of all time.

But officials close to the probe cautioned that this was merely "one of several theories." There was also the possibility of an explosion in flight due to a malfunction, one source said.

At least 17 Americans were listed among the dead.

Technicians were still sifting through the wreckage looking for clues as to what caused the crash of the DC10 Sunday, which killed all 346 persons aboard.

A policeman on the wooded site 23 miles north of Paris found part of one of the plane's two flight recorders, devices which record the functioning of the plane's main units. Another recorder, which copies down all conversation in the cockpit, was still missing.

"With the two recorders we may have a better chance of finding out what happened," said one expert. "For instance, whether the pilot had any advance warning of disaster."

There were reports that guerrillas carrying explosives might have been aboard the plane but the Turkish government said, "We have no official information on that," and that it was "impossible to know the cause of the crash at this point."

Speculation about a sabotage attempt was prompted by two facts, sources said.

Six bodies were found relatively intact six miles away from the main impact area in a forest. This indicated the bodies were ejected while the aircraft was still aloft, pointing to the possibility of an explosion in flight, they said.

And the main wreckage was so shattered it was likely the jet broke up before it hit the ground, the sources added.

Victims' clothing dangles from trees as photographers take pictures of the wreckage from the downed Turkish DC-10.

"But this is just one of several working hypotheses," one expert said. "It will be at least a week before we can say anything for sure."

A French newspaper and a news agency received phone calls during the night by a man claiming the crash was due to sabotage. He claimed to represent something called "The Liberal Front" and that the blast was a way of protesting against the French government, newspapers said.

Police officials said, however, the calls were probably from cranks and were not being taken seriously.

■ ■ ■

Further investigation showed that a faulty cargo door had blown off in flight, causing a loss of air pressure in the plane. The sudden decompression sucked six passengers through the open doorway and made the aircraft's floor break apart, severing the cables that controlled the DC-10's engine and flying controls. Just two years earlier a similar cargo-door mishap on another DC-10 almost resulted in a fatal crash. If U.S. officials and McDonnell-Douglas had taken extra safety precautions in 1972, the Turkish Airlines crash might not have happened. In 1975 the U.S. government ordered inspections of all DC-10s and similar planes, and McDonnell-Douglas made improvements on its cargo door latches.

KLM-Pan Am Runway Collision

**Santa Cruz de Tenerife, Canary Islands
March 27, 1977
Death Toll: 583**

The Canary Islands, controlled by Spain, are about 60 miles west of Morocco and a popular tourist destination. In 1977 one of the islands, Tenerife, was the site of the worst aviation disaster in history, which happened before the two planes involved ever left the runway.

March 28, 1977

Plane Crash Death Toll Hits 562

Reports On Cause Still Conflicting

SANTA CRUZ DE TENERIFE, Canary Islands (AP)—The Spanish air ministry said today the death toll from the fiery collision here of Pan American and KLM jumbo jets had climbed to 562 in history's worst aviation disaster.

There were conflicting reports on the cause of Sunday's collision. One report quoted airport sources as saying a misunderstanding by the American Pan Am pilot may have been a factor. But Spanish officials told a news conference the "key point of the investigation" was whether the KLM jet had permission to take off.

Officials said 72 persons survived the collision of the two Boeing 747s on the fog-shrouded runway. All the survivors were aboard the American plane, and 11 were listed in very serious or grave condition. All 239 on the Dutch plane were killed.

"The whole (American) plane was on fire and people were crying and screaming trying to get out," said James Naik, 37, of Cupertino, Calif. "Within just a few seconds the metal started to come apart."

The Spanish news agency Cifra quoted airport sources as saying the flight recorder from the American plane showed the airport control tower had ordered Pan American pilot Capt. Victor Grubbs of Centerport, N.Y., to move onto the main runway. The sources said the U.S. plane apparently misunderstood the order and taxied onto another runway where the KLM plane was taking off, Cifra said.

But Manuel de Prado, president of the Spanish national airline Iberia, said the KLM plane had been ordered to taxi to the end of the main runway, turn 180 degrees and prepare for takeoff. The Pan Am plane was told to follow down the runway and turn off onto a taxiway.

De Prado said he did not know whether the KLM plane had permission to take off. "This is the key point of the investigation," said Tenerife Gov. Antonio Oyarzabal.

Asked about a possible language problem, a spokesman for the control tower said the controllers talk to air crews exclusively in English.

In New York, a Pan American spokesman said the airline expected "anything substantive" concerning the cause of the collision to come from a U.S. government investigating team sent to the crash site "and anything else we view with concern."

Cifra quoted Grubbs, who was hospitalized at the Santa Cruz General Hospital, as saying he was taxiing down the main runway at the time of the collision.

"The crew saw nothing right up to the moment of impact," he was quoted as saying.

Another survivor, Roland Brusco Jr., of Longview, Wash., said the passengers were told the KLM jet was to hold its departure while the Pan American plane taxied across the runway to await its turn for takeoff.

"According to our pilot, the other plane was to hold at the other end of the runway," Brusco told the Portland Oregonian newspaper by telephone. "We pulled out and followed them. Just as we got to the offramp, where we would get out of the way, well, communications must have gotten mixed up."

He said the Pan American plane was taxiing when "all of a sudden we were turning and someone was screaming that KLM was taking off.… Everyone was screaming."

John Hackette of Nashville, Tenn., said his fiancee, stewardess Joan Jackson, told him the Pan Am pilot saw the other jet "and tried to get out of his way but it was too late."

Those who survived the holocaust of fire and explosions were thrown from the plane on impact or managed to scramble to safety before the flames filled the passenger compartment.

Wreckage is strewn across the Tenerife airport after the runway collision between two 747 jumbo jets in 1977.

One survivor, John Charles Amadour, 35, of Marina Del Ray, Calif., telephoned his father that "he looked out on the runway and saw the (KLM) plane coming right at him," his father said.

"He ducked down to put his head between his knees and he heard the grinding and the crash. He looked up and said the plane was split in three pieces.

"He felt as if he was in an oven. He said he was afraid he was going to be roasted…He was clamoring to get to this opening. Others were too. They were fighting and pushing. Finally he jumped about 12 feet, right into the rim of the fire and smoke, he landed on his back."

Investigators were en route to Tenerife from the United States, the Spanish mainland and the Netherlands to try to determine the cause of the collision. The U.S. Embassy in Madrid sent an eight-man delegation including a doctor, and three U.S. Air Force C130 transports were ordered from bases in the Canaries and West Germany to move the dead and injured....

■ ■ ■

When he saw the KLM plane barreling toward him, the Pan Am pilot managed to get his jet partially off the runway. That maneuver saved the lives of some of his passengers, but hundreds of other tourists were not so lucky.

March 30, 1977

Hangar Carpeted by Bodies

SANTA CRUZ DE TENERIFE, Canary Islands (AP)—Up close in the hangar, where the bodies lie in wall-to-wall rivers of blackened limbs, the statistics stop and the horror begins.

The 575 dead lie in two streams of burned bodies, each 50 yards long and five yards wide, that roll from one end to the other of a hangar at the edge of the runway.

More bodies, more parts of bodies than anyone could stand to count, more bodies than the eye could take in with a single glance, more bodies contorted, bent, and blackened than a dozen nightmares could conjure up.

Their terror kills the cold orderliness of the statistics that say "worst aviation disaster in history."

The bodies in the hangar, like those that hung from trees in the crash of the Turkish DC10 that took 346 lives near Paris in 1974, until now the deadliest of crashes, obliterate the accounting, the toting up, and leave only tragedy.

The yellow hangar is now a packaging plant for death. On each side of the building, Spanish authorities have set up long tables where men in white coats and plastic gloves take bodies that are intact and eviscerate them on the tables to slow decomposition.

On one side are the victims from the wrecked KLM plane, and on the other those from the Pan Am jet. They are carried up from the floor, sometimes with a paper bag containing articles that the

Spanish authorities think might belong to them, and then are placed in bigger plastic sacks or mahogany-painted coffins.

The coffins, stacked like banana crates, sit between and alongside the rows of bodies.

The work is torturous and slow. Even with more than 20 men on the job during an 18-hour day, the bodies won't start to be repatriated until Sunday.

On Tuesday morning, when fog and rain blotted out the view of the wreckage that still litters the runway, like the parched carcass of an animal alongside a railroad track, a man who described himself as an American from New York came to the hangar to look for the body of his sister-in-law.

"It's not good for you to go in," he was told by a Spanish air force colonel, who is helping to direct the operation at the morgue. "It will not help, I think. There is not much to see."

I promised my brother," the American replied.

■ ■ ■

Faulty communications led to the Tenerife disaster. The KLM pilot had been using the same radio frequency other pilots were using at the same time. Because of interference, the pilot received an incomplete transmission from the radio tower and thought he was cleared to take off.

American Airlines Crash

**Chicago, Illinois
May 25, 1979
Death Toll: 273**

The 1960 midair collision of two airliners over New York City remained the deadliest United States aviation accident for almost 20 years (see page 48). In 1978 a collision near San Diego set a new U.S. record for fatalities, with 144—but the death toll in that disaster was nearly doubled just eight

months later at Chicago's O'Hare International Airport, when an American Airlines jet crashed shortly after takeoff.

May 26, 1979

272 Die As Jetliner Crashes in Chicago

Air Toll Worst In U.S. History

CHICAGO (AP)—An American Airlines wide-bodied jet loaded with 272 persons on a Memorial Day weekend flight crashed nose first and broke apart in flames Friday just after takeoff from O'Hare International Airport. Authorities said all aboard were killed in the worst air disaster in U.S. history.

Seconds before the Los Angeles-bound DC-10 jetliner crashed, one of its three engines fell off and landed on the runway, said Chicago Fire Commissioner Richard Albrecht. He said Flight 191 hit nose first about a half-mile from the runway in an abandoned airfield in Elk Grove Township.

Lee Alfano, police chief of the nearby community of Des Plaines, said there were no survivors....

Rescue workers walked through the smoking rubble, marking bodies with 4-foot-high metal stakes topped by red, yellow and black streamers. The yellow streamers indicated two to three bodies, the red one body and the black five bodies. About 50 stakes had been set out.

Several persons on the ground were injured by debris, at least two of them seriously enough to require hospitalization.

As darkness fell, floodlights were brought to the crash site and rescuers and investigators said they would work through the night looking for bodies and clues.

Neal Callahan, public affairs officer for the Federal Aviation Administration in Chicago, said a recording of conversations between the pilot and the control tower indicated the tower knew on takeoff there was trouble.

"The only thing we do know for sure is that he didn't have time to talk to the control tower," Callahan said.

Asked by reporters whether the plane should have been able to fly with one engine missing, Callahan said:

"Yes, it should fly, no question about that, but that's one thing that will be determined in a further investigation." The National Transportation Safety Board sent investigators from Washington....

"Underneath the left wing was on fire. Stuff was coming out—like white vapor," said John Zuccaro, who saw the crash from the ground. "It had to be gas. It was coming out from the left wing. And the thing started turning over. As soon as it was turned over it was going down fast."

Firefighters try to douse flaming debris following the 1979 American Airlines jet crash shortly after the plane's takeoff from Chicago's O'Hare Airport.

Roy Mueller, manager of the Oasis mobile home park near the disaster site, said, "We heard a loud rumbling. We went to the door and we saw this airplane flip-flopping in the air. It bellied over and went straight down.

"One of my superintendents just came back from the field and he said, 'There's bodies scattered all over.'"

John Wayne, a Chicago area resident, was on an Ozark Airlines flight landing on another runway at the time American Flight 191 took off.

"The plane was in the air, and the young fellow in front of me said, 'Look at that.' I looked over and he said, 'The engine fell off.' We watched the plane as far as we could. He went on a fairly level course and gained just a little teeny bit of altitude and then he nosed off to the left, the wing went down and it was just one solid mass of flame all at once."

Robert Anderson was driving nearby when the plane crashed in an abandoned airfield in Elk Grove Township northwest of Chicago.

He said the plane was "almost vertical and I almost started to scream because I knew it would not come out of it."

"It continued almost upside down. As it impacted, flames shot out to where I thought my face was going to be singed," Anderson said. "When I looked back, it looked like an atomic bomb explosion."

Other eyewitnesses said the left engine came loose, and then the plane banked to the left, shuddered for a few seconds and struck the ground, hitting on its nose and left wingtip at about the same time.

Witnesses also said the plane appeared to be traveling at an unusually slow speed for a jetliner taking off.

Hospitals in the area were alerted to receive survivors, but the alert was soon canceled.

A temporary morgue was set up at an American Airlines hangar at O'Hare. Chicago police sent six paddy-wagons to help remove bodies.

Relatives of victims were asked to gather at a nearby high school.

Highways in the area were jammed with rush-hour motorists and hundreds of people gathered at the grisly scene, including residents of a nearby trailer park, some of whom suffered minor injuries from debris.

O'Hare, the world's busiest airport, shut down briefly, disrupting heavy holiday traffic, but later some runways reopened. Departing flights were delayed an hour or more.

After the crash, which occurred at 3:03 p.m. CDT under clear but windy skies, a United Airlines employee reported he could see flames from eight miles away....

■ ■ ■

May 28, 1979

Fracture of Bolt Let Engine Fall

CHICAGO (AP)—The fracture of a 3-inch-long bolt caused an engine to fall from the American Airlines DC-10 jetliner that crashed and killed 273 persons, the National Transportation Safety Board said Sunday.

But the loss of the engine alone should not have caused the crash, the safety board said, adding that its inquiry was continuing into the nation's worst aviation disaster.

Elwood Driver, vice chairman of the NTSB, said the board voted unanimously to recommend that similar engine-support systems on all DC-10s be inspected immediately.

An aerial photo shows the site where the American jet crashed just outside O'Hare Airport, located at the top of the picture.

Ray Towne, a spokesman for McDonnell Douglas, manufacturer of the DC-10, said in Long Beach, Calif., that the company asked 41 airlines to inspect their DC-10s within seven days.

He said there are about 275 DC-10s in service.

The Federal Aviation Administration, which could order such an inspection, called a news conference for this morning, and FAA spokesman Jerome Doolittle said Sunday night in Washington that the agency would announce a directive that probably would call for special inspections of many, and possibly all, DC-10s.

Art Jackson, spokesman for American Airlines,

said mechanics have inspected the engine-support systems of 12 of American's fleet of 30 DC-10s since Saturday. He said all were found "in good shape." He said the rest of the planes will be inspected by this morning.

The bolt—one of those connecting the wing to the pylon that carries the wing engine—was found 8,000 feet down the runway from where Flight 191 took off Friday, Driver said.

It was described as three-eighths to one-half inch in diameter and 3 inches long, and was broken in half.

All 271 persons aboard the jet died in the fireball crash, and two persons on the ground were also killed.

■ ■ ■

The cracking of the bolt on the DC-10's engine not only caused the engine to fall off but also affected the hydraulic lines that controlled the flaps on the left wing. The flaps help give the plane lift at low speeds. The problem with the flaps caused the plane to tilt violently and then crash.

Further investigation showed that American Airlines mechanics had not followed proper procedures when removing the engines for maintenance, leading to the problem with the engine bolt. The FAA was also criticized for failing to monitor the airline's maintenance practices.

In 1982 relatives of the victims won an $8.4-million legal settlement.

Air New Zealand Crash

**Mount Erebus, Antarctica
November 28, 1979
Death Toll: 257**

A pilot's attempt to give his passengers a spectacular view of a volcano led to the only major commercial-aviation disaster ever on the icy continent of Antarctica.

November 29, 1979

257 Die in Antarctic Crash

AUCKLAND, New Zealand (AP)—An Air New Zealand DC-10 carrying 257 persons on a sight-seeing flight to the bottom of the world slammed into a volcano Wednesday on the ice-bound coast of Antarctica, apparently killing all aboard. It was one of history's worst air disasters.

The 237 passengers on the flight included 20 Americans, according to a list of victims released by the airline today. Airline officials initially reported 12 Americans aboard.

A Navy C-130 search plane from the U.S. Antarctica base at McMurdo Sound spotted the wreckage in the sunlit polar midnight about 1,500 feet up the slope of Mount Erebus, a smoldering, 12,400-foot peak that is one of the world's tallest active volcanoes.

Three New Zealand mountain climbers were dropped by helicopter at the crash site today and reported seeing no sign of life. The tail portion of the giant plane was intact but empty, they said. A search party was on the way overland to the foot of the mountain.

The departure of the mountain climbers for the crash site was first postponed four to six hours due to bad weather, a Navy spokesman said. "There is a lot of blowing snow and it's just really nasty up there on Mount Erebus right now," the spokesman said. "We are working with great caution" in order to avoid another crash, said an ANZ spokesman in Christchurch.

The flight, advertised as a "trip to the end of the world," cost each passenger $340.

The harsh conditions of terrain, blowing snow and tricky 40-mph winds around the volcano kept Navy helicopters from McMurdo, 30 miles away on Ross Island, from landing at the crash site immediately.

A New Zealand Air Force C-130 transport carrying 28 persons including police identification experts, crash investigators, a government scientist, three journalists and two four-man teams of mountain climbers was scheduled to leave today for a New Zealand base near McMurdo Sound.

New Zealand Prime Minister Robert Muldoon said bodies would be taken to the base for identification, then flown back to New Zealand, weather permitting. "We will endeavor to get out as many as possible taking into consideration the safety factors," he said.

Erebus is on Ross Island, off the Antarctica coast 2,000 miles south of New Zealand. A low-altitude swing past the volcano is part of the spectacular 11-hour air tour.

The cause of the crash was not known.

A spokesman for the Department of Science and Industrial Research in Christchurch, New Zealand, said the plane appeared to have exploded when it hit the volcano.

Wreckage from the DC-10 litters the snowy slopes of Mount Erebus, an active volcano in Antarctica. The plane carried 257 people on a 1979 sightseeing flight over the volcano.

"The crew did not report any trouble in their last radio contact" at 2:30 p.m. Wednesday, Air New Zealand spokesman Chris Smith said.

The passenger list issued by the airliner indicated 56 of the 257 persons aboard were foreigners: 20 Americans, 24 Japanese, seven Britons, two Canadians and one person each from Switzerland, Australia and France. They paid $359 each.

The full identities of the victims, including 20 crew members, were being withheld until notification of next of kin, airline officials said. The list released included last names, but only first initials and no hometowns. One of the crew was well-known New Zealand mountaineer Peter Mulgrew, an associate of famed Mount Everest conqueror Sir Edmund Hillary, who gave the passengers a commentary on the sights.

The sightseeing planes fly from Auckland to Erebus and McMurdo Sound, cruise at a low level over that area, then fly for 45 minutes north along the Victoria Land coast before heading out across the water for the return to New Zealand. Air New Zealand has operated the flights for the last three Southern Hemisphere summers, and this was the fourth of the season.

At 8 p.m. Wednesday, the jetliner was reported an hour overdue for a refueling stop at Christchurch, and at 10 p.m. the airline declared it lost, saying its fuel would have been depleted by 9:30 p.m.

Because the last radio contact was from 38 miles north of McMurdo, the U.S. base sent up two ski-equipped Navy C-130s, a C-141 Starlifter and two Navy helicopters to conduct a search. The fire-blackened remains of the plane were finally spotted on the northern slope of Erebus, 30 miles north of the base.

"The wreckage was spread over an area of about 200 yards," said Hatcher, spokesman at the Navy Group Support Headquarters in Christchurch.

Smith said it was unclear whether the plane had just begun the tour or was headed northward to New Zealand when it crashed. But Hatcher said its position on the north slope indicated it was flying south.

"If the weather's nice, they come in at 2,000

feet or so to get a look at the volcano," Hatcher said of the aerial tours.

Smith said a report from the area—he was unsure whether it was from the pilot or the ground—said there was a slight cloud layer at about 3,000 feet.

Navy personnel reported temperatures had dipped Wednesday to about 15 degrees Fahrenheit in the area, where daylight is almost continuous at this time of year.

■ ■ ■

Captain Tim Collins, pilot of the DC-10, had descended from an altitude of 10,000 feet to about 2,000 feet, apparently to come in under the clouds obscuring the view of the volcano. In the initial news reports Collins was blamed for the crash.

November 29, 1979

Pilot Erred In DC-10 Crash

CHRISTCHURCH, New Zealand (AP)—The New Zealand DC-10 that carried 257 persons to their deaths in Antarctica was on the wrong side of the volcano it hit, and the pilot apparently was to blame, the director of the recovery operation said today.

Mountaineers who reached the slopes of Mount Erebus said a polar blizzard quickly was burying the bodies and wreckage, a U.S. Navy spokesman reported.

The death toll in Wednesday's crash was the fourth-largest in aviation history. Twenty-one Americans were among the victims.

Recovery operation director Roy Thomson said the Air New Zealand DC-10, on a sightseeing flight to the Antarctic, "was basically on the wrong side of the mountain."

"It would seem there has been a substantial error in navigation by the pilot.... It crashed on the northeast side of Mount Erebus. It should have been passing the mountain on the northwest side," said Thomson, chief of the Antarctica division of New Zealand's Department of Scientific and Industrial Research.

Thomson said he could almost certainly rule out the possibility of structural or mechanical failure.

"In my opinion the plane was certainly in the wrong place to come down so low," Thomson, one of the country's foremost authorities on the Antarctic, told reporters in Auckland, New Zealand, before leaving to head up operations to try to recover the bodies.

Recovery of the bodies from the frozen Antarctica coast 2,000 miles south of here will be a formidable task. The plane crashed and exploded about 1,500 feet up the side of the 12,400-foot Erebus, an active volcano.

Two rescue workers stand by the wheels of the DC-10 that crashed into Mount Erebus. The wreckage covered an area about as large as six football fields placed end to end.

A three-man New Zealand mountaineering team lowered to the crash site by U.S. Navy helicopter reported no sign of survivors. They sighted "60 or 70 bodies," but the bodies were fast being covered by blowing snow on the permanent ice pack, the Navy spokesman said.

The New Zealanders reported subzero temperatures and said blizzard-like winds were blowing pieces of wreckage down the mountainside, crisscrossed with deep crevasses.

The reports to a Navy headquarters here were made by radio from the U.S. research base at McMurdo Sound, some 40 miles from Erebus. Both the mountain and the base are on Ross Island, just off the coast.

The Navy spokesman said the mountaineers, who made two trips to the site, will try to build a shelter as a base for recovery operations.

He said they would map the wreck site and await the arrival of a 28-man New Zealand recovery team, including police identification experts, crash investigators and two four-man mountain climbing teams. They were to fly in to McMurdo Friday aboard a New Zealand Air Force C-130 Hercules transport.

Prime Minister Robert Muldoon said the bodies recovered would be taken to Scott Base for identification, then flown to New Zealand.

■ ■ ■

A later investigation determined that part of the plane's navigational system had probably malfunctioned, since Collins was an experienced pilot and the crash came with almost no warning from the plane's safety systems.

Only about one-third of the 257 bodies were recovered from the snow-covered side of Mount Erebus.

Passenger-Train Derailment

Mansi, India
June 6, 1981
Death Toll: more than 500

The world's worst train accidents have occurred during wartime, and in the past governments often restricted press reports of such disasters, especially if they had military implications. In 1917, during World War I, more than 500 French soldiers died in a train derailment, and in 1944, during World War II, an Italian train disaster killed more than 500 people as well. A 1981 railroad accident in India ranks with those two among the world's worst ever.

June 8, 1981

400 perish in India rail disaster

NEW DELHI, India (AP)—More than 400 people are missing after a packed passenger train toppled off a bridge, a railway official said today. An Indian news agency said the train jumped the tracks to avoid hitting a cow, the animal held sacred by India's Hindus.

"The train had a capacity of carrying 500 passengers and only 67 were rescued," national railways spokesman S.G. Purohit said. "The coaches were fully used and some people were traveling on the roofs."

A rail car sits on the bank of the Bagmati River after rescuers retrieved it from the waters. Other debris from the deadly 1981 train derailment lies near the car.

The chief minister of Bihar State, Jagannath Mishra, said the accident was the "biggest and worst in living memory" in India

Purohit said navy divers had recovered 48 bodies from the rain-swollen Bagmati River near Mansi, 248 miles northwest of Calcutta, where seven of the train's nine coaches plunged Saturday night. Only one of the seven coaches had been located, he said.

The United News of India said injured passengers reported the train toppled into the river when the engineer braked suddenly in a windstorm to avoid hitting a cow on the rusty tracks of a bridge.

The railway minister gave a different explanation, saying the train was "blown off" the bridge by a fierce gale. The Railway Ministry denied reports that the old 1,464-foot bridge collapsed and tumbled the train into the river.

"There has been no damage to the bridge or the tracks," said the ministry.

The train was en route from Samastipur to Banmakshi.

The United News said the engineer fled after the disaster.

Navy divers searched the waters and recovered 46 bodies, Pande said. The Press Trust of India news agency said rescue workers had not reached six cars that were carried downstream.

Seven cars plunged into the river, while the locomotive and one coach were left hanging from the bridge.

Reports from the scene said more than 10,000 people went to the bridge, many of them weeping, to inquire after relatives. Authorities set up tent camps at the site to feed and shelter the crowd.

■ ■ ■

Uncertainty about the cause of the wreck and the death toll continued for days. The most likely explanation for the crash was the sudden braking of the train.

June 9, 1981

Deaths Mount in India Wreck

Associated Press

NEW DELHI, India—Divers recovered 215 bodies and continued to search the area where a packed, narrow-gauge train that may have been carrying thousands of passengers plunged into the Bagmati River, the United News of India reported.

Various government officials said thousands may have perished in the crash, which would make it history's worst railroad disaster.

Seven cars of the 10-car train went off a bridge Saturday near Mansi, 248 miles northwest of Calcutta. The cause of the accident was unclear.

Railway officials said Monday that more than 500 people were on the train and only 83 had been found alive. A spokesman said the train was filled to capacity and was carrying an undetermined number of people on the coach roofs.

Gajendra Prasad, deputy assembly speaker of Bihar state, where the accident occurred, said the train was so overcrowded the death toll could be as high as 3,000, the Press Trust of India reported.

R.V. Paswan, leader of the opposition Lok Dal Party, demanded Prime Minister Indira Gandhi's government resign for failure to prevent the accident on the government railway system. He said more than 2,500 probably died, UNI reported.

UNI said 165 of the bodies were found near the bridge and 50 were discovered 2.4 miles downstream. There will be a mass cremation on the banks of the river, it said.

The bodies were recovered by Indian navy divers and army salvage crews, who had located only four submerged cars by Monday night. More divers were due to arrive today, along with heavy salvage gear from navy shipyards.

Fatal railway accidents have occurred frequently in India, but Saturday's river disaster was so serious that Gandhi ordered India's top navy commander, Adm. R.L. Pereira, to the scene, UNI said.

The minister of railways and other officials said a fierce gale blew the seven wood-and-metal cars off the bridge, leaving only the locomotive and two cars on the rails.

Paswan and several other people who visited the scene disagreed with the government's explanation. They said there was no sign of damage to nearby buildings from winds violent enough to blow a train off its tracks, UNI said.

The news agency said weather stations in the area recorded no gales or thunderstorms at the time of the disaster.

Choudhury Saladdin, the state rural development minister, blamed the accident on "sudden application of the brakes," causing derailment. Injured survivors have been quoted as saying the driver braked suddenly to save a cow, a buffalo or a herdsman standing on the track. Railways spokesman S.G. Purohit refused to comment.

History's worst recorded rail accident was the derailment of a troop train in the Alps at Modane, France, in 1917, killing 550 people. The second worst was the suffocation of 521 occupants of a train stalled in a tunnel near Salerno, Italy, in March 1944.

■ ■ ■

Divers eventually recovered 268 bodies from the Bagmati River, but more than 300 people remained missing and were presumed dead, which would make this the highest death toll for a train accident. Because of the uncertainty of the death count, however, some sources still list the 1917 French rail disaster as the world's deadliest.

Korean Air Lines Shootdown

Over Sakhalin Island, the Soviet Union
August 31, 1983
Death Toll: 269

After the election of President Ronald Reagan in 1980 relations between the United States and the Soviet Union were sometimes strained. Reagan had called the Soviet Union an "evil empire," and he pushed for huge increases in U.S. defense spending. The two countries continued to negotiate regarding the control of nuclear weapons and were planning talks for late 1983. Those talks were almost derailed after a Soviet military attack on a Korean jetliner.

September 1, 1983

Airliner downed by Soviets

Korean jumbo jet felled by missile

Associated Press

A Soviet jet fighter shot down a South Korean jumbo jet carrying 269 people after tracking it for more than 2½ hours when it strayed over the Soviet island of Sakhalin, Secretary of State George P. Shultz said today. He said the United States "reacts with revulsion" and has demanded an explanation.

One of the passengers was Rep. Larry McDonald, D-Ga., chairman of the John Birch Society. McDonald had boarded the flight only because he had missed an earlier one by minutes, and aide reported.

Shultz said the aircraft strayed into Soviet airspace and was tracked by the Soviets for more than 2½ hours. He said that as many as eight Soviet fighters were involved in the affair.

Korean war veterans burn a Soviet flag during a demonstration protesting the 1983 downing of Korean Air Lines Flight 007 by a Soviet jet fighter.

In New York, officials of Korean Air Lines said today they did not believe their jet had strayed off course. They also said the plane would have landed if it had been ordered to do so. Y.S. Lee, general manager of the New York office, said there was no indication the plane went off course into Soviet space.

"At 1826 hours, the Soviet pilot" of one plane "reported that he fired a missile and the target was destroyed," said Shultz.

Shultz said that about an hour later a Soviet pilot reported seeing kerosene near the surface where the plane went down. He said there was "no excuse whatsoever for this appalling act."

Shultz told reporters at the State Department that President Reagan had been informed.

Shultz said that Richard Burt, the assistant secretary of state for European affairs, summoned the Soviet charges, Oleg M. Sokolov, this morning to "express our grave concern" and to "demand an explanation."

Sokolov heads the Soviet Embassy here in the absence of Ambassador Anatoly F. Dobrynin, who is in Moscow.

Shultz also said there was no evidence the Soviets had warned the plane, although he said the plane that fired the missile "was close enough for a visual inspection."

He also said, "As far as we could see, there was no communication between the planes."

Shultz gave the following account of the events and aftermath of the downing of the plane:

1400 GMT, Wednesday (10 a.m. EDT), the airliner left from a refueling stop at Anchorage.

1600 GMT, noon EDT, the aircraft "came to the attention of Soviet radar" and was tracked constantly by the Soviets thereafter. It strayed into Soviet airspace over the Kamchatka Peninsula, over the Sea of Okhotsk and over Sakhalin Island.

1812 GMT, a Soviet pilot reported visual contact with the airliner.

1821 GMT, the Soviet pilot reported the plane at 10,000 meters.

1826 GMT, "the Soviet pilot reported that he fired a missile and the target was destroyed."

1830 GMT, the Korean aircraft was reported by radar at 5,000 meters.

1838 GMT, the Korean plane disappeared from radar screens.

Pentagon sources said the fighter that shot down the Korean jetliner was a MiG-23.

The Korean plane, a Boeing 747, was bound from Anchorage, Alaska, to Seoul, South Korea, when it dropped off Japanese air control radar, Pentagon sources said earlier.

The Japanese asked for U.S. help in searching for the plane and two patrol aircraft were sent aloft from Misawa Air Force Base in Japan and from Okinawa during the night, according to Pentagon officials.

The Korean jetliner was last heard from at 2:23 p.m. EDT Wednesday.

The United States responded to the downing by sending five F-15 fighter planes to Misawa, near the northern tip of the main Japanese island of Honshu, Pentagon sources said.

The MiG-23 is one of the Soviet Union's most advanced jet fighters. It is armed with air-to-air missiles code-named by NATO as "Aphid" and "Apex."

The Soviet fighter is capable of speeds in excess of 1,600 miles per hour and has a combat radius of up to 745 miles from its home base.

Earlier this week, Japan's defense agency reported that the Soviet Union has stationed more than ten MiG-23s on Etorofu Island, one of four former Japanese islands occupied by the Soviet Union at the end of World War II.

This island is about 150 miles east of the northernmost Japanese island of Hokkaido.

The last time anything like this occurred was in April 1978 when a South Korean Boeing 707 en route to Seoul from Paris over the North Pole with a refueling stop in Anchorage went off course and was fired on by Soviet fighters and forced down on a frozen lake in the Soviet Union.

Two passengers were reported killed and two others seriously injured in that incident. No Americans were aboard that plane.

At the time, the Soviet Union said the surviving passengers and crew would be released.

Three days after the South Korean plane was forced down about 230 miles south of Murmansk in the Soviet Arctic—more than 1,000 miles off its course—the Soviets released 106 passengers and bodies of a Japanese and a Korean passenger, but detained the pilot and navigator for questioning.

Soviet officials in Moscow said later that the jetliner trespassed in Soviet airspace for more than two hours and ignored a variety of warnings, including tracer shells fired in front of it.

At least one shell hit the airliner, killing two of the passengers and wounding 13 others, two of them seriously.

■ ■ ■

Some Soviet officials denied their fighters shot down the KAL plane. Finally, as the Americans and Soviets exchanged accusations, the Soviets did admit to downing KAL 007, but they claimed the jet was on a spy mission.

September 9, 1983

Body, debris found from airliner

By The Associated Press

A child's body and a fragment from the tail of the downed South Korean airliner have been found on the coast of northern Japan, authorities said today.

Glass and metal fragments were embedded in the body found by fishermen, leading police to believe the youngster may have been a passenger aboard the plane the Soviets shot down.

The body, missing its legs and the top half of its head, was found Thursday about 100 yards off the coast of a peninsula on the northwest coast of Hokkaido, Japan's northern island.

A medical professor who examined the body said the child was between 6 and 11 years old, but the skin had deteriorated so badly that the child's race could not be identified, police said.

An autopsy was being conducted this evening, but police said the body had a metal fragment in the head and glass splinters in the chest, which indicated the child may have been aboard the plane.

Among about 20 pieces of debris that washed ashore in two days was a piece of metal measuring about 30 inches by 36 inches, painted red, and bearing the white letter "L" and part of another letter, police said.

A Korean Air Lines representative here, Park Chung-hong, identified the fragment as coming from the downed Boeing 747, and said the vertical tail pieces of all KAL jetliners are painted red and have the while letters "HL," followed by four numerals.

The fragment was found Friday morning at Hamatonbetsucho, a town 39 miles southeast of here, police said.

The fragment and other metal and sponge-like pieces of debris were being sent to Tokyo for further analysis, police said.

Meanwhile, a top Kremlin general said today a U.S. spy plane rendezvoused with the South Korean airliner that entered Soviet airspace on Washington's orders and ignored at least 120 warning shots before a Soviet warplane destroyed it with a missile.

"The plane obviously must have been flying toward Soviet airspace fulfilling a spy mission…. Why did it proceed in no other place than the one with Soviet installations?" asked Marshal Nikolai V. Ogarkov, the Soviet military chief of staff.

About three weeks after KAL 007 was shot down over Sakhalin Island, U.S. warships search for sunken wreckage.

In a rare news conference at the Soviet Foreign Ministry televised overseas, Ogarkov told foreign reporters that Soviet defense forces detected Korean Air Lines Flight 007 flying side by side with an American RC-135 surveillance aircraft for 10 minutes near a sensitive Soviet military zone in the Sea of Japan, 310 miles off the jetliner's intended course.

"Their flights were certainly coordinated so as to make our task more difficult and confuse our air defense forces," the marshal said.

He said the South Korean Boeing 747 later tried to flee when interceptors scrambled to meet it and defied the 120 warning shots before a Soviet warplane blasted it with an air-to-air missile.

This was the first Soviet acknowledgment that one of its planes downed the South Korean jetliner with a missile, one of two Ogarkov said were fired. Previously, the Soviets had said only that the flight was "stopped."

On the warning shots, Ogarkov said Soviet pilots fired two sets of warning shots, including a series of "four bursts" totalling 120 rounds of tracer shells.

The United States has admitted that an RC-135 spy plane was in the area the day of the shooting, but claims it was never closer than 300 miles to the jetliner and was on the ground in Alaska one hour before the jetliner was shot down....

■ ■ ■

The Soviets retrieved the wreckage and black box from the plane; ten years later the black box was turned over to the International Civil Aviation Organization (ICAO). In the meantime, the ICAO had concluded that the Soviets had not tried to make radio contact with the jet to warn the pilot that he had strayed. The organization also found that all navigation equipment on KAL 007 had been working properly, and the crew was not aware that the plane's flight pattern would take it over Soviet airspace.

Almost immediately after the downing of the KAL plane many people theorized that the shooting was not accidental. A 1996 book, *Incident at Sakhalin,* suggests the Korean plane was deliberately flying off course and was actually destroyed off Honshu, the main island of Japan. The U.S. government, however, considers the case closed and believes the plane was shot down accidentally, as the ICAO determined.

Despite the heated words exchanged after the disaster, the United States and the Soviet Union continued their negotiations on nuclear weapons, though the talks ended later that year without any agreements to reduce arms.

Japan Air Lines Crash

Mount Ogura, Japan
August 12, 1985
Death Toll: 520

The worst air disaster ever involving a single plane took place in Japan, when a modified Boeing 747 crashed into a mountain.

August 13, 1985

4 survive crash fatal to 520

3 other survivors reported found

KITA-AKAMURA, Japan (AP)—A Japanese jumbo jet packed with 524 people crashed in rugged mountains of central Japan on Monday. Unconfirmed reports said there were seven survivors of what was believed to be the worst single-plane crash ever.

Nagano prefectural (state) police were quoted as saying at least four people—two women, an eight-year-old girl and a boy—were found alive in the wreckage.

Japan Broadcasting Corp. and Kyodo News Service reported today that three more survivors had been found, but gave no further details about them. The Nagano police, the National Police Agency and a JAL spokesman said they had no information to confirm that report.

Television networks showed pictures of a young girl and an older woman on stretchers, battered and bandaged. Police identified them as Mrs. Hiroko Yoshizaki, 35, and her daughter, Michiko Yoshizaki, 8, and said they and the other woman survivor, Keiko Kawakami, were flown by military helicopter to a hospital in Fujioka city, 25 miles west of the crash scene.

The boy was reported still trapped in the wreckage.

Three dozen helicopter-borne troops made a rope descent into steep, thickly forested mountain country this morning to reach the wreckage of the Japan Air Lines Boeing 747.

The jetliner crashed on a domestic flight from Tokyo to Osaka. The pilot, Masami Takahama, 49, had reported a door was broken, that he was fighting for control and would try an emergency landing.

Hiroshi Ochiai, a Self Defense Force spokesman, earlier said initial reports from the crash site, at about 5,000 feet, indicated no survivors among the 509 passengers and 15 crew members aboard.

JAL spokesman Geoffrey Tudor said two Americans were on the passenger list. They were identified as Edward Anderson, believed to be 48, and Michael Hanson, 40, both employees of Stearns Catalytic Co., of Denver, Colo. Neil McLagan, a Stearns vice president, confirmed Anderson and Hanson were on the airplane.

The jetliner crashed at about 6:54 p.m. (5:54 a.m. EDT), on the north side of Mount Ogura, a 6,929-foot peak about 50 miles from Yokota and 70 miles northwest of Tokyo.

The site is in a remote area in a range known as the Japan Alps. The only roads in the region follow river valleys that cut through steep, densely forested mountainsides.

The tail section of the Japan Air Lines jet burns after the plane crashed on Mount Ogura in August 1985.

In Seattle, Wash., Boeing spokesman Bill Mellon said a five-member team of company investigators would leave today for Japan. In Washington, D.C., Ed Pinto, a Federal Aviation Administration spokesman, said FAA investigators might be sent if Japanese officials requested them.

Tudor said JAL Flight 123 left Tokyo's Haneda Airport bound for Osaka carrying 509 passengers, including 12 infants, and a crew of 15.

It left Haneda at 6:12 p.m. It had been scheduled to leave at 6 p.m. and to arrive at Osaka, less than 250 miles away, at 7 p.m.

Tudor said that at 6:36 p.m., the plane reported: "Rear 5 door broken, making emergency descent."

Judging from the communication, he said: "It appears the aircraft crew had difficulty controlling the aircraft."

Seiichiro Kondo, a spokesman for Nagano state police, said 1,000 police, firefighters and Self-Defense personnel were searching for the missing plane.

A live Japan Broadcasting Corp. telecast from a helicopter over the site showed pieces of still smoldering, widely scattered wreckage. Japan Air Lines markings were clear on some of the debris, but no survivors or bodies could be seen.

Keizo Shimizu of the Transport Ministry said Takahama, a veteran pilot with more than 12,000 hours flying, requested radar guidance from Tokyo air control at 6:25 p.m. while descending to 22,000 feet. Air control officials told the plane to proceed 90 degrees east.

Takahama declared an emergency two minutes later, he said. At 6:28 p.m., traffic control told the pilot again to fly 90 degrees east, instead of northwest, but Takahama only responded, "Unreliable control."

Shimizu said traffic control asked Takahama if he could land in Nagoya, about 165 miles west of Tokyo, and he said he wanted to head back to Haneda.

At 6:46 p.m., Takahama said "Unreliable control" or "Unable control," Shimizu added, and when air control asked if he wanted to land at Haneda, he shouted, "Yes, please proceed with that!"

Traffic control confirmed the plane's location as 51 miles west of Haneda. At 6:55 p.m., both Haneda Airport and Yokota Air Base gave the plane permission for an emergency landing, Shimizu said, but there was no further communication from the 747. Yokota is a major American military base about 20 miles west of Tokyo.

In 1974, the crash of a Turkish DC-10 near Paris killed 346 people. In 1977, the runway collision of two 747 jumbo jets killed 582 people at Tenerife, in the Canary Islands.

Most aircraft are loaded to capacity at this

time of year, when families traditionally gather at ancestral homes to pay respects to their ancestors.

JAL said the plane was a 747SR, a Boeing model configured for large passenger loads on relatively short flights. The SR stands for short range.

Dozens of weeping relatives gathered at Haneda and at the airport in Osaka to await word on possible survivors. Most of the passengers came from the Osaka area. Four busloads of passengers' families left Tokyo Monday night for the site.

JAL released a passenger list that included 21 non-Japanese names, and Tudor said there were two Americans, two Italians, one Briton, one West German and four Chinese residents of Hong Kong.

News reports said the passenger list included Kyu Sakamoto, a popular singer known internationally for his 1961 hit record, "The Sukiyaki Song." It was not confirmed that he was aboard, however.

Kyodo News Service quoted witnesses as saying they saw the plane make a long, sweeping turn and then saw "red and black flames."

■ ■ ■

August 15, 1985

Survivor: 'big noise' before crash

FUJIOKA, Japan (AP)—A Japan Air Lines jumbo jet pitched wildly and there was a "big noise" 35 minutes before the airliner slammed into a mountain with 524 people aboard, a survivor of history's worst single-aircraft disaster said.

The account by Yumi Ochiai, 26, an off-duty JAL stewardess, was released by the airline Wednesday. Only four people are known to have survived Monday's Boeing 747 crash.

From her hospital bed, Mrs. Ochiai told JAL officials that after hearing the noise about 35 minutes before the crash, "the ceiling above the lavatories came off, the oxygen masks came down, and an announcement came on for people to put on their face masks."

She said the crash itself was a series of "three jolts," accompanied by a swirl of seats and cushions. She said the next thing she knew, a helicopter was flying overhead.

Five representatives of the Boeing Commercial Airplane Co., builders of the jumbo jet, and four U.S. officials, two each from the Federal Aviation Administration and the National Transportation Safety Board, were in Tokyo to join Transport Ministry investigators. They were expected to focus on how the tail section of the plane became disabled before the craft slammed in Mt. Osukata.

The charred remains of the Japan Air Lines jet's fuselage lie partly buried on the mountainside.

Unless more survivors are found, the death toll will stand at 520, far exceeding the toll of 346 in the worst previous single-plane disaster, the crash of a Turkish DC-10 near Paris in 1974.

A collision of two jumbo jets on the ground in the Canary Islands in 1977 killed 582 people.

Three days after Monday's crash, rescuers had found 141 bodies and confirmed the identities of 73, said a police official at rescue headquarters. He would not give his name.

A police spokesman at the recovery operation's local command post said there was only the "remotest chance" of finding more survivors.

JAL President Yasumoto Takagi told reporters Wednesday he would resign to accept responsibility for the crash. He said he would step down when the accident investigation appeared settled.

An airline spokesman said the jetliner was also involved in a 1978 accident, when it received "minor damage" to its tail section. But the airline said all the damaged parts had been replaced by Boeing.

■ ■ ■

The JAL jet might have received only "minor damage" during its 1978 accident, but apparently the repairs to fix that damage contributed to the 1985 crash. A metal bulkhead separating the passenger cabin and the plane's tail section had been fastened with only a single line of rivets, not the double line called for in Boeing's repair manuals. Seven years later the rivets gave way, and the plane lost part of its tail section in flight.

Arrow Air Crash

**Gander, Newfoundland, Canada
December 12, 1985
Death Toll: 256**

Four months after the JAL crash in Japan (see page 75) America's holiday season was darkened by the news of another fatal air disaster.

(see page 75)

December 12, 1985

250 GIs die in jet crash

Associated Press

GANDER, Newfoundland—A DC-8 charter carrying about 250 U.S. servicemen from the Middle East home for Christmas burst into flames and crashed today shortly after takeoff from Gander International Airport, killing all aboard, officials and witnesses said.

The plane was carrying members of the 101st Airborne assigned to the Sinai peacekeeping force back to Fort Campbell, Ky., where the unit is headquartered, the Pentagon said. It had stopped in Cologne, West Germany, for refueling.

The Pentagon said there were more than 250 military personnel aboard, but no dependents, from the division, which had been on peacekeeping duty since July.

Maj. Kenneth Miller of Canadian Search and Rescue reported in a telephone interview from Halifax, Nova Scotia, that 250 passengers and eight crewmembers were killed in the crash.

Miller said, "All we know is that there were no survivors." He said his information came from the Gander control center.

CBC radio correspondent at the scene, Ed Pike, quoted witnesses as saying the plane exploded, lighting up the sky.

While firemen search for bodies, the landing gear of the Arrow Air DC-8 burns after it crashed in Gander, Newfoundland.

"We were driving to work…when we saw this big explosion…and it dived down very quickly. In a matter of seconds, it was gone," said Ann Hurley, a nearby resident.

The Hopkinsville (Ky.) New Era reported Wednesday that a detachment of more than 200 soldiers from the 3rd Battalion, 502nd Infantry, 101st Airborne Division, was due at the local post today at 9 a.m. CST (10 a.m. EST).

Federal Aviation Administration spokesman Vedder Steed in Atlanta, Ga., said the plane belonged to Arrow Air, a Miami-based charter firm.

Gander airport manager John Pittman said the plane went down about a quarter-mile from the airport.

When asked if there was a fire aboard, he said "yes," but did not elaborate.

Roads to the airport were blocked as emergency vehicles made their way to the scene.

In Ottawa, a Transport Canada spokesman said a crash operations center was set up at about 6 a.m., about 45 minutes after first word of the crash was received.

The airport was overcast with light snow and light winds at the time of the crash, according to the aviation weather report. There had been light, freezing drizzle a few hours earlier.

Gander International Airport is located approximately 150 miles northwest of St. John's, the capital of Newfoundland, on Canada's Atlantic seaboard. It often is used by planes traveling between North America and Europe....

■ ■ ■

During the next few days, as steady snowfall blanketed Gander, investigators rushed to find parts from the plane. In the United States some people wondered if the plane had been sabotaged by terrorists to protest the U.S. presence in the Middle East. American officials dismissed that theory. Instead, most attention focused on possible mechanical failures as the cause of the crash.

December 15, 1985

Crashed Jet Had History Of Problems

Associated Press

MIAMI—Arrow Air officials confirmed Saturday that the chartered DC-8 that crashed in Canada, killing 256 people, experienced mechanical difficulties earlier this year and had to abort two takeoffs in the past six months.

On a Nov. 15 flight from Grand Rapids, Mich., the jet's nose lifted into the air but quickly settled back onto the runway after the tail hit the ground, said Robin Mattell, spokesman for Miami-based Arrow Air.

On that flight, the plane was carrying 99 Marine reservists from Grand Rapids to Camp Lejeune, N.C., on a weekend emergency mobilization drill, Mattell said. He said a "loading problem" at the rear of the plane was believed to have caused the incident.

After stopping, the airplane successfully took off and competed its flight without incident, Mattell said.

The engine and part of a wing from the Arrow Air DC-8 lie in rubble following the 1985 crash.

On July 28, the same DC-8 was carrying members of the Kentucky Guard and Ohio Air National Guard when forced to abort a takeoff from the Toledo, Ohio, airport, he confirmed.

Mattell said reports that there was an explosion and an engine fire were incorrect.

"There were some mechanical problems, but there was no fire or explosion," he said.

Mattell said he did not know the nature of the difficulties. After a delay at Toledo, the plane flew to Bangor, Maine, and West Germany without further problem.

"I want to emphasize that we have never flown an airplane that was not completely safe to fly," Mattell said.

The DC-8 crashed Thursday while taking off from Gander, Newfoundland, on a flight from Cairo, Egypt, to Fort Campbell, Ky., headquarters of the 101st Airborne Division. The crash killed all eight crew members and 248 U.S. soldiers who had been on peace-keeping duties in the Sinai Desert.

They were the first fatalities for Arrow Air.

Mattell said the airline has flown 40 million aircraft miles and logged 85,000 hours of flight time in its four-year history.

However, Arrow Air had a number of safety violations in 1984 and last summer agreed to pay a $34,000 fine for record-keeping that did not meet FAA requirements....

■ ■ ■

Officials from both Canada and the United States investigated the crash and decided two factors probably played a part. For some reason—either human negligence or a mechanical problem—one of the plane's four engines was not at full power. Also, the crew had underestimated the weight of the plane's load by 6 tons.

A congressional hearing on the operations of Arrow Air showed that the company had a history of performing minimal maintenance and often made its crews fly long hours. In the past the charter line's pilots had even fallen asleep in the cockpit.

Arrow filed for bankruptcy in 1986.

Explosion of the *Challenger*

Over Cape Canaveral, Florida
January 28, 1986
Death Toll: 7

After the success of the Apollo moon missions the National Aeronautics and Space Administration (NASA) turned its attention closer to Earth. In 1981 NASA launched the first space shuttle, *Columbia,* with two astronauts on board. The shuttle was a reusable spacecraft designed to let astronauts conduct scientific experiments in the weightlessness of space. Ultimately, NASA planned to use the shuttle to build a permanent space station above Earth.

By 1986 shuttle missions were becoming routine, just as NASA had hoped. Three different shuttles made a total of five flights in 1985, and the crew for the first mission of 1986, in the *Columbia,* included Bill Nelson, the first congressman to fly

in space. The year's second mission, using the shuttle *Challenger,* had another special passenger: Christa McAuliffe, a public-school teacher and the first "average citizen" in space.

As millions of Americans watched the launch on TV, *Challenger* blew apart in a sickening explosion.

January 29, 1986

Nation mourns 7 heroes

Probers gathering to find out why shuttle blew apart

Vessels and aircraft comb ocean for debris

By Howard Benedict
AP Aerospace Writer

CAPE CANAVERAL, Fla.—Ships and aircraft searched the sea today for debris from shattered Challenger and the remains of the five men and two women who died in a "national tragedy" that dealt a severe setback to America's space program.

An investigation team was to meet today to start the long probe into why the $1.2 billion spaceship, seemingly on a perfect course, suddenly blew apart 74 seconds after liftoff Tuesday, raining fiery debris into the Atlantic Ocean.

Some experts who studied television tapes of the disaster said they thought the problem centered in the external fuel tank, containing more than a half-million gallons of liquid hydrogen and oxygen to power the orbiter aloft.

The deaths were the first aloft after 55 successful U.S. man-in-space flights, including 24 previous shuttle missions. The first "common citizen" chosen for a space trip, New Hampshire schoolteacher Christa McAuliffe, was one of the victims.

"We mourn seven heroes," a somber President Reagan told the nation.

Reagan delayed for one week his State of the Union speech, which had been scheduled for Tuesday night, and ordered American flags to be flown at half staff through Monday on public buildings and military installations.

Eight ships, including four Coast Guard cutters, searched throughout the night over the 50-

by-100-mile rectangle where Challenger's wreckage fell. Eight planes and helicopters resumed their hunt at daylight.

Lt. Joe Carr of the Coast Guard, which is coordinating the search, said several small pieces of wreckage drifted ashore in the Cape Canaveral area overnight. He asked residents who find anything that might be a part of the shuttle to turn it in to the Coast Guard.

Coast Guard vessels also picked up debris of varying sizes overnight, but Lt. Cmdr. Jim Simpson could offer no specifics.

Simpson said search ships spotted what they described as "floating tanks." But because of darkness and the fear of an explosion from volatile residue, the ships did not attempt immediately to recover the items, he said.

Earlier, a few pieces "five or 10 feet long" were spotted, but most of the recovered items were thermal tiles, about 30,000 of which covered the shuttle to protect it from reentry heat, said Col. John Shults, director of Defense Department contingency operations.

The search area is between 50 and 130 miles southeast of Cape Canaveral, the water between 70 and 200 feet deep. Although the explosion occurred 10 miles high and 8 miles southeast of the launch pad, the shuttle's nearly 2,000 mph momentum propelled the wreckage much farther out over water.

The debris will be examine in a hangar at nearby Patrick Air Force Base.

The investigation could take months, just as it did after America's only other space program tragedy, the launch pad fire that killed three Apollo astronauts 19 years ago this week. The Soviets have lost four cosmonauts in flight.

The Apollo fire, in a test, grounded astronauts for 21 months, and Tuesday's explosion is expected to halt space shuttle flights for many months. Jesse Moore, director of NASA's shuttle program, said a shuttle will not fly again until the cause of the accident is pinpointed and corrections made.

The National Aeronautics and Space Administration had planned a record 15 shuttle flights this year, and Challenger was on the second. The ship, making its 10th flight, had been the workhorse of a four-ship fleet.

Killed along with McAuliffe were commander Francis R. Scobee, 46; pilot Michael J. Smith, 40; Judith A. Resnik, 36; Ronald E. McNair, 35; Ellison S. Onizuka, 39; and Gregory B. Jarvis, 41.

A photo taken before the 1986 liftoff of the space shuttle Challenger *shows a puff of smoke coming from the craft's faulty rocket booster.*

Scobee, Resnik, American's second woman in space, McNair, the nation's second black astronaut, and Onizuka, a Japanese-American, were making their second shuttle flight. Jarvis, an employee of Hughes Aircraft, was on the trip to conduct fluid dynamics tests developed by his company.

At the president's request, Vice President George Bush flew to Cape Canaveral to offer condolences to the families of the astronauts, who watched in horror as Challenger was transformed into a raging fireball.

There was no immediate explanation for the accident.

Mission Control reported there had been no indication of any problem with the shuttle's three main, liquid-powered engines, its twin solid-fuel rocket boosters or any other system. Officials said the shuttle just suddenly blew apart and that radio data ceased at 74 seconds.

The absence of any concrete radio information could hamper the investigation, especially if no large parts of the destroyed shuttle can be recovered. In the case of the Apollo fire, the spacecraft was on the ground, and the evidence was there to examine.

"Data from all the shuttle instrumentation, photographs, launch pad systems, hardware, cargo, ground support systems and even notes made by any member of the launch team and flight ops (operations) team are being impounded," said shuttle director Moore.

He named an interim investigation team headed by Kennedy Space Center director Richard Smith, and said NASA acting administrator William R. Graham would soon name a formal review board.

"At 11:40 a.m. this morning, the space program experienced a national tragedy," Moore said.

The explosion occurred as Scobee was throttling the main engines back to maximum thrust after dropping them to 65 percent to reduce forces of gravity on the ship. It took place just after the spaceship drove through an area where wind and other atmospheric forces exert maximum pressure on its outside.

■ ■ ■

On the morning of the launch the temperature at Cape Canaveral had dropped to 27 degrees Fahrenheit. By launch time it had risen only slightly above freezing. As the government commission studying the *Challenger* disaster learned, the low temperature, along with lax safety measures, played a big part in the explosion.

June 9, 1986

Challenger report pinpoints seal, lack of safety margins

By DAVID ESPO
Associated Press Writer

WASHINGTON (AP)—The destruction of Challenger and the death of its seven crew members had a single cause—the failure of a seal in the shuttle's booster rocket, the Rogers Commission said today. Its report faulted NASA for operating a "silent safety" program that concealed festering problems with the seal from top launch managers.

The panel urged NASA to review all items whose performance are deemed critical to shuttle flights and said the orbiter's tires, brakes and steering systems "do not have sufficient safety margin."

In its report to the president, just over four months after the Jan. 28 disaster, the commission said Challenger "struggled futilely against forces" triggered immediately after ignition when gas leaked past the seal.

Managers Unaware

The commission said the shuttle should not have been launched, and wouldn't have been if top launch managers had been aware of opposition from rocket engineers who feared the effects of cold temperatures.

"If the decision-makers had known all of the facts, it is highly unlikely that they would have decided to launch," the commission said.

In a 256-page report that combined a millisecond-by-millisecond dissection of the Challenger accident with sweeping recommendations for improved safety and management practices, the panel also said the shuttle's crew "apparently had no indication of a problem before the rapid breakup" of the craft 73 seconds into flight.

No Alarms

"There were no alarms sounded in the cockpit," where the seven astronauts rode, or in Mission

Control. "There was nothing that either the crew or the ground controllers could have done to avert the catastrophe," concluded the panel.

Although the commission called for many changes in NASA's practices, the final report singled out the Marshall Space Flight Center, the facility which oversees the booster rocket program. The report said Marshall suffers from "management isolation" which needs to be eliminated "whether by changes of personnel, organization, indoctrination or all three."

The report said NASA's highly successful safety program—a "hallmark during the Apollo program"—was allowed to lapse, and no where more than at Marshall.

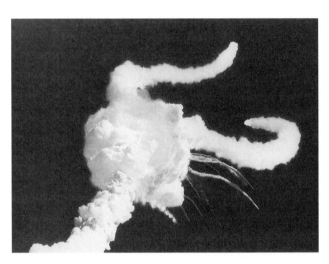

Trails of smoke fill the sky over Cape Canaveral following the space shuttle Challenger's *explosion 74 seconds after takeoff.*

Unfactual Testimony

The panel also pointedly criticized Lawrence Mulloy, the NASA official who was in charge of the solid rocket motor program at the time of the launch, for providing testimony that was contradicted by other facts developed in the case.

The commission, headed by former Secretary of State William P. Rogers, arranged to formally present its report to President Reagan at early afternoon. NASA Administrator James Fletcher, who has scheduled a news conference for later in the day, already has implemented some of the commission's recommendations.

Rendering its verdict on the nation's worst space disaster after a 120-day probe, the commission demanded that NASA change the design on the solid rocket boosters. "No design options should be prematurely precluded because of schedule, cost or reliance on existing hardware," the commission said.

Tests Suggested

It added that NASA should give "full consideration" to conducting test firings on a redesigned rocket in a vertical configuration, a plan that some NASA officials have said previously could delay the return of the shuttle to space well beyond the July 1987 target date....

■ ■ ■

The *Challenger* explosion set back the shuttle program for two years. The next shuttle mission was launched on September 29, 1988. *Discovery,* redesigned after the recommendations of the Rogers Commission, carried five astronauts on a successful five-day mission. It would take another six years, however, for the shuttles to fly as regularly as they had before the *Challenger* disaster.

Dona Paz-Victor Collision

Tablas Strait, the Philippines
December 20, 1987
Death Toll: 1,600–3,000 (estimated)

The Philippines are composed of more than 7,000 islands, and for people who can't afford air travel ferries are the most common form of transportation between the islands. Unfortunately, safety has not always been a major concern for the companies that run the country's ships and ferries. From 1972 until June 1987, 117 ships sank in Philippine waters, 53 had fires on board, and 80 collisions were reported.

A December 1987 collision between the ferry *Dona Paz* and a tanker led to a huge maritime disaster.

Ships collide; 1,490 missing

Fire erupts on ferry off Philippines

Associated Press

MANILA, Philippines—Shipping sources said 1,490 people were listed as missing and feared drowned after the collision of a passenger ship and an oil tanker Sunday night. Both vessels sank.

The sources, who spoke on condition of anonymity, also said at least 26 people were rescued. An earlier report said 27 had been rescued.

The collision between the 2,215-ton MV Dona Paz and the Philippine oil tanker MT Victor occurred about 10 p.m. Sunday, said Eusebio Go, general manager of the Sulpico Lines. The accident happened off Marinduque island, 100 miles south of Manila, he said.

Bong Meneses of the Philippine Rescue Coordinating Center said both vessels sank and that the passenger vessel burst into flames. Most of the survivors were plucked from the water by a passing merchant vessel, he said.

Go said he was uncertain how many people were aboard the passenger liner but that its capacity was listed at 1,424 passengers. He did not know how many crew members were aboard. Survivors said the passenger vessel was jammed.

It was not immediately clear how many people were aboard the oil tanker.

Cmdr. Rene Luspo, spokesman for the Philippine coast guard, said two naval patrol ships and four commercial vessels had been sent to the scene.

The Dona Paz had been expected to arrive in Manila at 4 a.m. today. Go said the shipping company was uncertain about details of the accident because it had not made radio contact with the ferry since about 8 p.m. Sunday.

Lt. Jose Cabildo of the Philippine coast guard said the Victor was bound for Masbate island with 8,300 barrels of oil. Survivors said the passenger vessel was filled with people heading for Manila for the Christmas holidays.

Most of the survivors suffered burns when they jumped into the flaming water, officials said.

Samuel Carillo, one of the survivors, told the Associated Press he was walking to the ship's canteen after a chat with the captain when he felt "a jerk and an explosion."

Villagers gather around dead bodies that washed ashore on the Philippine island of Mindoro after the 1987 Dona Paz collision. Local fishermen placed the victims in the sacks.

"I went up and there were flames all over, and I jumped," he said.

Another survivor—42-year-old Paquito Osabel—said he was on his way to Manila with his sister and three nieces to spend Christmas with his family.

He said the vessel was so crowded that up to four people were sharing individual cots, and hundreds of others were sitting on the floor of the three-deck ship. Osabel said he was chatting with his relatives, all of whom are missing, when he heard an explosion.

"I went to a window to see what happened, and I saw the sea in flames," he said. "And I shouted to my companions to get ready, there is fire. The fire spread rapidly and there were flames everywhere. People were screaming and jumping. The smoke was terrible. We couldn't see each other and it was dark. I could see flames, but I jumped."

Alodia Bacsal, 18, said panic broke out on the vessel. "People were screaming and running," she said. "Then all of a sudden there was smoke everywhere." Her father, Salvador, was also rescued, but her grandfather and uncle were missing.

■ ■ ■

Although the _Dona Paz_ was designed to carry about 1,500 passengers and crew, many people reported that the ship was actually packed with more than twice that many people. If, indeed, more than 3,000 people had been on board, then the sinking of the _Dona Paz_ would be the 20th century's worst peacetime disaster at sea.

After the crash and fire survivors recounted their nightmarish experience.

December 22, 1987

Survivors recall 'sea in flames' after Dona Paz catches fire

Associated Press

MANILA, Philippines—The Dona Paz sailed through the calm water, running lights gleaming, taking 1,500 people to Manila for Christmas. Then there was a jolt, an explosion and, as Paquito Osabel said: "I saw the sea in flames."

Panic-stricken passengers screamed the names of loved ones as smoke and fire engulfed the ship, and the ones who saved themselves jumped into the blazing oil-slick water.

The last moments Osabel spent with his sister and three nieces was when they had settled cross-legged on the floor on one of the crowded ship's three decks. He was taking the women to spend Christmas with his family in Manila.

It was 10 p.m. Sunday, 18 hours after the five boarded the Dona Paz at Tacloban City on Leyte island. In six more hours, it was to dock in Manila.

The inter-island passenger ship carried 1,493 passengers and crew, said the owners, Sulpicio Shipping Lines. But it was so crowded with holiday travelers that up to four people shared individual cots.

Suddenly there was a violent jar followed by a loud explosion.

"I went to a window to see what happened, and I saw the sea in flames," Osabel said in a Manila hospital. "I shouted to my companions to get ready. 'There's a fire!' I said.

Relatives load coffins of some of the victims from the Dona Paz *onto a Philippine navy ship.*

"The fire spread rapidly and engulfed our ship. There were flames everywhere. People were screaming and jumping. The smoke was terrible. We couldn't see each other and it was dark. I could see flames on the water below, but I jumped anyway."

Osabel, 42, said he never again saw his sister Alejandra, 56, and his nieces Evangelina, Anna Liza and Loreta. "I don't know where they are," he said. "We were to spend Christmas with my family here."

He was among only 26 people rescued from the 2,215-ton Dona Paz and the Philippine oil tanker Victor. Both sank immediately after colliding off Mindoro Island, about 110 miles southeast of Manila.

Another inter-island ship, the Don Claudio, picked up 24 Dona Paz passengers and two tanker crewmen….

Alodia Bacsal, 18, and her father, Salvador Bacsal, 44, were among those rescued. She said her grandfather, an uncle and a cousin were missing.

Alodia Bacsal was severely burned on the face and other parts of the body. Her father had burns on the face.

"People were screaming and running," she said. "Then all of a sudden there was smoke everywhere. I jumped into the sea and there were flames all over."

Her father said: "I went to look for my daughter, who was also shouting for me. Suddenly smoke filled the ship and it was hard to breathe." He said an undertow pulled him away from the blanket of fire.

■ ■ ■

The next day about 115 additional bodies were found. A few days later the coast guard had its first inkling of what had happened on board the *Dona Paz* before the accident. An apprentice sailor was alone on the bridge steering the ship through the Tablas Strait, a busy waterway. The ship's officers, including the captain, were either watching TV or drinking beer at the time at the time of the collision.

Iran Air Shootdown

Over the Strait of Hormuz
July 3, 1988
Death Toll: 290

The countries of Iran and Iraq are two of the largest producers of oil in the world. During most of the 1980s these Middle Eastern nations waged a bloody war over which country controlled the Shatt al-Arab, a waterway separating the two countries. Given the importance of oil to Western countries, the United States and European nations wanted to ensure the Iran-Iraq war did not disrupt the flow of oil out of the Persian Gulf.

In 1987 an Iraqi fighter jet damaged the U.S.S. *Stark,* a frigate patrolling the gulf, killing 37 sailors. The plane had been warned to stay away from the ship but then fired a missile from 10 miles away. The ship had no chance to defend itself. Iraq called the incident an accident, but the missile attack showed the need for U.S. Navy captains to be alert in the gulf. The captain of the *Stark* was reprimanded for not properly defending his ship.

The next year a skirmish between American and Iranian forces broke out in the gulf. Perhaps remembering the *Stark,* the captain of the U.S.S. *Vincennes* was ready for an attack. Unfortunately, a commercial airliner became an accidental casualty of that military encounter.

July 4, 1988

U.S. downs Iranian jetliner

Reagan defends military's action, 'deeply regrets' loss of 290 lives

Associated Press

WASHINGTON—President Reagan declared Sunday that the U.S. downing of an Iran Air jetliner was "a proper defensive action," and Pentagon officials said Navy officers believed they were fending off an attacking Iranian fighter that ignored seven warnings.

Reagan called the incident a "terrible human tragedy" and said, "We deeply regret any loss of life." The incident occurred on the second of two days of skirmishes between Iran and the United States through the Strait of Hormuz, at the mouth of the Persian Gulf.

The Islamic Republic News Agency said the plane, a commercial Airbus carrying 290 people from the Iranian port of Bandar Abbas to Dubai, was hit by two U.S. missiles and that all aboard were presumed dead.

Adm. William Crowe, chairman of the Joint Chiefs of Staff, said there had been a visual sighting as the missiles hit the craft and that eyewitnesses had seen the craft "disintegrate." He said the incoming craft had not been visually identified when the missiles were fired, but defended the commander who he said ordered the firing in the belief his ship was in jeopardy.

Crowe said it had been thought the incoming aircraft was an Iranian F-14 fighter, the most lethal plane owned by Iran.

The U.S. ship which fired was the USS Vincennes, an Aegis class cruiser equipped with sophisticated radar and missiles.

The airliner was four or five miles outside the commercial corridor between Dubai and a joint civilian-military airfield at Bandar Abbas, and flew directly at the Vincennes as the U.S. warship exchanged fire with several of Iran's Boghammer gunboats, said Crowe.

The Vincennes and a smaller U.S. frigate, the USS Elmer Montgomery, firing 5-inch guns, sank two Iranian patrol boats and damaged a third, Pentagon officials said. The number of victims aboard the Iranian boats was not known.

No American casualties were reported.

Tehran Radio, monitored in Cyprus, was quick to react to the incident. "America's crime today in downing an Iranian Airbus is…new evidence of American crimes and mischiefs, crimes which expose America's nature more than ever before," it said.

The Pentagon early Sunday announced that the Vincennes had shot down an Iranian F-14, but hours later sources told The Associated Press that military officials had come to believe the identification of the craft was wrong. At 1:30 p.m. EDT. Crowe appeared before reporters to say he believed the downed aircraft was a civilian airliner.

As Crowe spoke, Reagan—in a statement read by spokesman Marlin Fitzwater—promised a full investigation by the Defense Department.

Reagan said the Iran Air jet was headed directly for the USS Vincennes.

"When the aircraft failed to heed repeated warnings, the Vincennes followed standing orders and widely publicized procedures, firing to protect itself against possible attack," Reagan said in his statement.

Crowe expressed "deep regret" over the loss of life, but emphasized time and again that the military commanders in the Persian Gulf had "acted with good judgment" in that they believed American ships were being approached by a hostile aircraft.

As the aircraft approached the Vincennes, it dropped in altitude and accelerated to about 450 knots, as a warplane would do if preparing to fire an anti-ship missile, Crowe said.

Those actions and electronic transmissions "led us to believe it was a military aircraft," he said.

In the seven minutes between the detection of the aircraft on U.S. radar and the firing of the missiles, Crowe said, the U.S. warship "sent three warnings on a civilian distress network and four warnings on a military distress network."

A crewman of the Iranian tug Hirmand *holds a piece of wreckage (right) from the Iran Air jet shot down by the U.S. cruiser* Vincennes *in 1988.*

The Iranian aircraft "neither answered nor changed its course," he said. "There were electronic warnings on the Vincennes that led it to believe the aircraft was an Iranian F-14," but which Crowe described as classified and refused to discuss. Most civilian aircraft emit signals identifying themselves and monitor specific civilian radio frequencies.

When the Iranian aircraft was "about nine miles away, the Vincennes fired two standard surface-to-air-missiles, at least one of which hit at an approximate range of six miles," Crowe said.

Crowe said he did not intend to imply that Iran sent the airliner into the combat zone on purpose, but said "if a country's going to wage combat operations in a certain area and then send a commercial airliner in there during that, of course it's an accident waiting to happen."

In his statement, Reagan said, "I am saddened to report that it appears that in a proper defensive action by the USS Vincennes this morning in the Persian Gulf an Iranian airliner was shot down over the Strait of Hormuz.

"The only U.S. interest in the Persian Gulf is peace and this tragedy reinforces the need to achieve that goal with all possible speed," Reagan said.

Meanwhile, European and Latin American governments said the incident showed the urgent need for peace in the region, but they stopped short of criticizing the United States.

In London, British Prime Minister Margaret Thatcher expressed regret for the "tragic accident" but said U.S. forces had the right to defend themselves.

"This has been a tragedy for all concerned," Thatcher said in a statement. "We understand that in the course of an engagement following an Iranian attack on the U.S. force, warnings were given to an unidentified aircraft apparently closing with the U.S. warship, but these warnings received no response."

■ ■ ■

The *Vincennes* incident was immediately compared to the Soviet Union's 1983 downing of a KAL jet (see page 72), but as in that shooting, the two sides involved in this disaster had different interpretations of what happened. The Italian navy, which had ships nearby, partially confirmed the American explanation. The Italians had heard radio transmissions from the *Vincennes* warning the Iranian jetliner to change course, but the commercial craft did not respond. Meanwhile, the Iranian government insisted that there had been no warning, and that the Americans had known the plane was a commercial airliner.

Relations between the United States and Iran had been poor ever since the 1979 Iranian hostage crisis (see Volume 2, *Civil Unrest and Terrorism*). The U.S. had supported Iran's

former leader, the dictatorial Shah Reza Pahlavi. When an Islamic fundamentalist government came to power, it took 52 Americans hostage and held them for more than a year. Tensions remained high even after the hostages were released. Now the Vincennes incident further fueled Iran's hatred of America.

July 6, 1988

Heir to Khomeini urges terrorist attacks on U.S. targets

Associated Press

NICOSIA, Cyprus—Iran told the world Tuesday the U.S. Navy created "a wave of rage" by shooting down an Iranian jetliner, and the designated heir to power urged terrorist attacks on American targets around the world.

Tehran radio quoted President Ali Khamenei as saying in letters to heads of state that Iran has the "right to avenge the blood of innocent children, men and women." Iran said all 290 people on the Iran Air flight were killed when the Airbus A300 was shot down Sunday.

"While the U.S. leadership has not yet officially declared its war against Iran's people, it has, by resorting to this criminal act, which followed earlier aggressive actions, taken a serious step toward war with a revolutionary, Islamic nation," he said.

Khamenei asked other nations to condemn the United States for the action by the U.S. missile cruiser Vincennes, which he said "roused a wave of rage in Iran."

At the United Nations in New York, Iran demanded a Security Council meeting, condemnation of the United States for the "terrorist attack" and withdrawal of U.S. military forces from the Persian Gulf, where Iran and Iraq have been at war since September 1980.

The radio said Ayatollah Hussein Ali Montazeri, designated successor to revolutionary patriarch

Ayatollah Ruhollah Khomeini, urged him in a letter to order "revolutionary cells…inside and outside Iran…to unleash their wrath on American financial, political and military targets everywhere."

He said Iran must "ignite a fire which will burn America and its lackeys."

Mourners carry coffins in the streets of Tehran during a mass funeral for the victims of the downed Iran Air jet.

In other developments:

• A six-man team of U.S. experts led by an admiral arrived in the gulf Tuesday to begin a confidential investigation. U.S. officials said the airliner was mistaken for an Iranian F-14 jet fighter.

• Iranian Ambassador Mohammad Ja'afar Mahallati told a news conference at the United Nations that Iran Air Flight 655 had sent "normal signals…to all radar that it was a civilian plane." The Pentagon said Tuesday it transmitted information on two radio channels, one "identified with F-14s."

• Air traffic to the United Arab Emirates was disrupted. Iran Air canceled its daily flights from Bandar Abbas to Dubai and said it would not use the corridor "threatened by the American naval presence." Dubai canceled flights of other airlines using the same corridor over the Strait of Hormuz.

■ ■ ■

Despite its tough talk, Iran did not unleash a new wave of terrorism against the United States. About a week after the shooting U.S. officials agreed to compensate the families of the victims, though the country did not admit any legal liability. The Iran-Iraq war ended the following month, as Iraq agreed to a cease-fire negotiated by the United Nations.

United Airlines Crash

Sioux City, Iowa
July 19, 1989
Death Toll: 111

The worst airplane crashes end with all or most of the passengers and crew killed. When a DC-10 carrying almost 300 people had an engine failure and then suffered a complete loss of its controls, the resulting crash could have been one of the worst disasters in American aviation history. Instead pilot A.C. Haynes made an emergency landing, and more than half the people on board survived the fiery crash.

July 20, 1989

195 feared dead in jet crash

Many still walk away after plane cartwheels

By MELISSA JORDAN
Associated Press

SIOUX CITY, Iowa—A United Airlines DC-10 carrying 298 people crashed Wednesday in a ball of fire and cartwheeled down a runway after the pilot tried to make an emergency landing.

An estimated 185 to 195 people died, Fire Chief Bob Hamilton said. But other officials said at least 125 survivors were taken to hospitals. There was no explanation for the discrepancy in numbers.

Flight 232, from Denver to Philadelphia via Chicago, carried 287 passengers and 11 crew members, said Deborah Jones, a United spokeswoman.

The plane crashed on an inactive runway at Sioux Gateway Airport after circling for about 30 minutes as pilots told passengers to prepare for a crash-landing, survivors said. The accident could be the second-worst U.S. air disaster.

The 15-year-old plane had "complete hydraulic failure" before it crashed just after 4 p.m., said Fred Farrar, a spokesman for the Federal Aviation Administration. The tail engine failed, and may have caused the hydraulic failure, said Bob Raynesford, another FAA spokesman....

This aerial view shows where the United jet skidded off the runway during an emergency landing at the Sioux City, Iowa, airport in 1989.

Passenger Charles Martz said there was no panic after the pilot calmly told passengers about the problem.

"The pilot got on and said one of our engines had blown and quit. He said when it blew it hurt the tail of the plane and the pilots couldn't control the plane," an unidentified survivor told radio station KMNS in Sioux City.

"We circled around for about a half-hour while the pilots figured out what to do," the survivors said. "Then they said we were preparing for a crash landing. They said it would be about 30 seconds, but it was about five minutes."

Cliff Marshall of Columbus, Ohio, who was returning home from Denver, said: "The plane came down. It bounced twice, flipped into the air and we were sitting there upside down and it began to fill up with smoke."

"Then God opened a hole in the basement [the bottom of the plane] and I pushed a little girl out. I grabbed another, kept pulling them out until they didn't come no more."

Marshall said he thought he helped a half-dozen get out before he ran.

Sixty people, 10 or 11 of them critically injured, were taken to St. Luke's Regional Medical Center and no others were expected, said James Hamilton, vice president for medicine. Injuries included burns, shock and broken bones.

"The amazing thing is that I heard that a number of people walked away from the accident," he said.

Sixty-five people were taken to the Marian Health Center, said Tom Chapman, a spokesman. "We also understand there are a number of walking wounded who will be coming in...."

■ ■ ■

July 21, 1989

Drama lived out aloft, monitored on ground

Associated Press

Lori Michaelson lowered her 1-year-old daughter to the floor between her knees and, like all of her fellow passengers aboard United Flight 232, assumed the crash position—bent at the waist, braced for sudden impact....

The DC-10 jet, crippled by a loss of hydraulic power, attempted an emergency landing at Sioux Gateway Airport. It rolled to its right a few feet from the ground, scraped its right wing and cartwheeled before bursting into flames.

Michaelson and her husband, Mark, managed to bring two of their children from the plane, but the force of the crash had pulled 1-year-old Sabrina from her mother's grasp.

Mark Michaelson's effort to return to the plane was blocked by heavy smoke but then they saw

Sabrina, apparently unharmed, in a woman's arms. The woman said a man had handed the girl to her.

"God, I wish he hadn't," said Mark Michaelson. "I'd like to thank him personally."

Here is the sequence of events, based on reports from officials of the National Transportation Safety Board, the FAA and press accounts. Times are EDT.

• 2:45 p.m., the United flight left Denver with 282 passengers, including three infants, a cockpit crew of three and eight flight attendants en route to Chicago.

• 4:16 p.m., the pilot reported to air traffic control in Minneapolis that the jet had lost one of its three engines and that he was losing altitude and having difficulty controlling the aircraft.

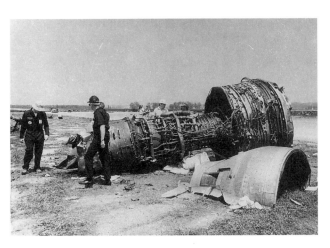

Two days after the Sioux City crash, federal investigators examine one of the burned engines from the ill-fated United jet.

• 4:17 p.m., flying at 31,000 feet, the pilot reported "complete hydraulic failure." On a jet, the hydraulic system powers vital control surfaces on the wings and tail that direct the plane's attitude and direction of flight, as well as controlling brakes on landing.

Air traffic control directed him to Dubuque, on Iowa's eastern edge.

• 4:20 p.m., the pilot declared an emergency, and controllers rerouted him to Sioux City, about 400 miles west of Dubuque.

• 4:40 p.m., the pilot told his passengers the tail section was damaged and the plane was en route to Sioux City for an emergency landing....

• 4:58 p.m., Flight 232 crashed into a cornfield just short of a runway, burst into flames and skidded into an adjoining cornfield....

With the advance warning, emergency medical and rescue crews were already at the scene.

Dr. David Greco, director of emergency services for the Marian Health Center, was one of the first physicians to arrive.

Dozens of people already were walking away from the wreckage, while others remained inside, handing out children to those on the ground.

"They all remained so calm, the ones that were talking and alert were calm and sane," Greco recalled. "They'd say, 'Go help someone else, I'm OK.'"

■ ■ ■

Despite the initial reports of a death toll approaching 200, the actual number was lower. Some of the survivors walked away from the crash with no injuries.

From his hospital bed Captain Haynes spoke tearfully about the passengers killed, but the governor of Iowa and other dignitaries praised Haynes for his actions. Other pilots said it was a miracle Haynes could even land the plane using just his engines to steer the craft.

TWA Explosion

Off the Coast of Long Island, New York
July 17, 1996
Death Toll: 230

In the 1990s terrorism came to the United States as it never had before. Middle Eastern terrorists set off a bomb at New York's Word Trade Center in 1993 (see Volume 2, *Civil Unrest and Terrorism*). Two years later three Americans were charged with blowing up a federal building in Oklahoma City (see Volume 2, *Civil Unrest and Terrorism*). Other terrorist attacks on U.S. targets had been thwarted before they were carried out. Many people thought terrorists had struck again when a TWA plane just minutes out of Kennedy Airport in New York exploded and plunged into the ocean.

July 18, 1996

229 die in crash

TWA flight from JFK explodes off Long Island

Associated Press

NEW YORK—A TWA jetliner with 229 people aboard exploded in a fireball shortly after taking off for Paris and plunged into the waters off Long Island on Wednesday night. There was no sign of survivors.

The 747 jet, Flight 800, was bound for Charles de Gaulle Airport from Kennedy Airport when it went into the Atlantic Ocean 20 miles off Moriches Inlet at about 8:45 p.m. The site off the south shore of the island is about 40 miles east of New York City.…

Signs of the explosion apparently could be seen from as far away as the Connecticut shore, including West Haven, Guilford, Madison, Clinton and Westbrook.

There were 212 passengers and 17 crew members on the flight, according to Mike Kelly, a TWA vice president. He said the plane had arrived from Athens, Greece, and had been on the ground about three hours before taking off for Paris. Some of the passengers were on board from an earlier canceled flight to Rome.

"We are not finding any survivors," said Steve Sapp of the U.S. Coast Guard. "We are locating lots of bodies out there."

From the air, wreckage and fuel on the water could be seen burning.

An 82-foot Coast Guard vessel out of New London was dispatched Wednesday night to aid in the rescue effort.

Suffolk County Fire Department Chief Myles Quinn said a temporary morgue was set up near the scene.…

Federal law enforcement agencies cautioned that it was too early to speculate on causes of the explosion or the crash. The FBI field office in New York City reportedly was on alert and consulting with aviation officials.

Airplane wreckage from TWA Flight 800 floats in the Atlantic Ocean off Long Island, New York, as rescue workers pull personal items belonging to the victims from the water after the 1996 explosion.

Asked about the possibility of a bomb, Federal Aviation Administration spokesman Eliot Brenner said "we can't discuss security issues.…"

In-air explosions can be caused by a variety of causes, including a bomb, a mid-air collision, an engine explosion that hits a fuel tank, structural failure or a roaring hazardous material fire such as the one that apparently brought down ValuJet Flight 592 on May 11.…

■ ■ ■

Articles about the victims soon filled the press. A group of sixteen students from Pennsylvania was on board for a vacation in France. One man was carrying an engagement ring to propose to his fiancée in Paris. These stories appeared alongside reports of the mystery surrounding the accident. A terrorist's bomb or mechanical failure was the most likely cause of the TWA crash. Some eyewitnesses, however, said they saw a white streak approach the plane before the explosion, and so a third possibility arose: a missile attack. The attack could have been deliberate, by terrorists, or the accidental firing of a U.S. missile. Officials hoped finding the plane's black box would help answer all the questions.

Divers find black boxes from TWA jet wreckage

Pace of search leaves families very frustrated

Associated Press

EAST MORICHES, N.Y.—Divers searching the wreckage of TWA Flight 800 found the flight data and cockpit voice recorders Wednesday.

The boxes were found shortly before midnight by a robotic vehicle probing the largest concentration of wreckage on the ocean floor, said Robert Francis, the vice chairman of the National Transportation Safety Board.

Divers were bringing the boxes to a Navy search vessel on the surface, and Francis said they would be flown immediately to Washington for examination. He did not say exactly where in the wreckage the boxes were found or their condition.

The recovery, coming one week after the crash, represented a major breakthrough in the quest to find out what caused the second-worst airline disaster in U.S. history.

Investigators expect the so-called black boxes—which are actually orange—to provide crucial evidence as to what caused the 747 to explode in a fireball and plunge into the Atlantic Ocean July 17, killing all 230 aboard.

The voice recorder picks up cockpit conversations and could indicate whether the crew knew if there was a problem before the crash and what action, if any, was taken to try to avoid the crash.

The flight data recorder picks up such information as a plane's altitude, speed and various equipment functions. It could help determine whether a mechanical problem brought the plane down.

But Al Dickinson, the NTSB's lead investigator, cautioned the boxes may not hold all the answers.

"I think this is going to add to our informa-tion, but it's not going to be a solving of every-thing, unfortunately," Dickinson said.

Until the discovery, the salvage effort was most notable for what it had not found. The FBI has not determined whether the jetliner was downed by a bomb, a missile or mechanical failure....

Almost two weeks after the mysterious explosion on board TWA Flight 800, a U.S. Navy diver swims through the plane's submerged debris. The salvaged pieces of the jet were brought to a nearby naval hangar for inspection.

Meantime, three more bodies were brought ashore earlier Wednesday. Of the 230 people who were killed, 116 bodies were still missing. Of the bodies recovered, 95 have been identified by the Suffolk County Medical Examiner's office.

Divers also believe they have spotted seven more bodies in the wreckage, Francis said....

■ ■ ■

The black box did not provide any conclusive evidence of what had happened. For the next few months Navy divers searched the ocean for pieces of the plane. The FBI could not say what had caused the accident, though rumors continued to circu-late that a U.S. missile had struck the jet. Government officials strongly denied this, and over time they said it was less likely that terrorists had brought down the plane. In May 1997 FBI director Louis Freeh said that mechanical failure was the most likely cause. The leading theory was that some sort of spark set off an explosion in the jet's center fuel tank.

Glossary

Astronaut A person trained to make flights in outer space.

Bathyscaph A small underwater vessel capable of diving several miles below the ocean's surface.

Black box The nickname for an electronic device that records the operations of an airplane; the data recorded is often useful in determining the cause of an aviation disaster.

Bulkhead A section of a ship that can be sealed to prevent the spread of water during a disaster.

Coach A railroad car that carries passengers.

Cosmonaut Russian term for an astronaut.

Dirigible An airship filled with gases that are lighter than air, enabling the craft to rise off the ground.

Federal Aviation Administration (FAA) Formerly the Federal Aviation Agency; U.S. government group that oversees air safety.

Maritime Relating to the sea.

Radar Acronym for "radio detecting and ranging"; a device that uses radio waves to determine the position of an object.

Satellite A small unmanned spacecraft that orbits Earth.

SOS A call for help during an emergency.

Set Index